**FOR THE MOST IMPORTANT WOMEN IN MY LIFE:**
*my mom Rose Mesquita, my sister Vivianne Mesquita and my daughter Bella Wierson, who helped me become the proud woman that I am today. I could not forget my dad Flavio Mesquita and my brother Flavinho Mesquita, who had a huge part in making me feel strong and certainly helped build my self-confidence. THANK YOU ALL! I LOVE YOU! AMO VOCÊS!*

# Contents

# Introduction

I always had a passion to inspire, support and empower other women. I grew up in Brazil, raised by a mother who is a very strong, beautiful and loving woman. She always taught my sister and me to feel good about ourselves the way we are, respect others, and help each other. My sister is my best friend. I had great women role models in my life. My first boss was a woman. Ruth Kjar was a Danish super dedicated professional, another very strong female personality, who was always pushing me forward and supporting my career. One female boss, however, was not very nice to me when I was pregnant, because she was younger, not married and, I believe, she didn't understand what it was to be a mother. It was not an easy situation back then, but life took care of teaching her what was right from wrong. I didn't have to do anything. A couple of years later, while she herself was pregnant, and law suits continued to pile up against her, she was fired. Life hands us hard lessons... hopefully she learned a good lesson and started seeing life with different eyes. That is how I believe life works, if you focus on being positive, follow your morals and your values, and choose how you react to your dark feelings in a positive way, life will take you to the places you want to go. Maybe I was lucky, but all that background, just created in me the desire to "pay it forward" and help women feel good about themselves personally and professionally. I always did it informally in my day to day life, and in a big way with my daughter, who is now a beautiful human being at 14 years old! I think life gave me a girl as a child so that I could "pay it forward" in a more profound way!

Last year, February 2018, at 46 years old, while I was searching for my next career move, I decided to put in motion a way to reach a bigger number of women to inspire and empower, in a more organized manner through an Instagram account I called @FeelFabulousByFabiana. Two women supported me and pushed me to go forward with this idea: my sister Vivianne Mesquita and my Brazilian friend Renata Stephens, over a coffee during a cold winter day in Minneapolis. At the beginning, I was sharing tips on Fashion, Fitness and Health, but then I felt I wanted to share more! I wanted to touch these women in a deeper way. Really making them think about themselves, about how they could live their lives better, be happier being who they are. So, I started writing motivational quotes almost every day. I got inspired by books, articles, movies, real life situations, to write the messages I posted. I am not going to be able to remember exactly where or what inspired each quote. Some of them I actually credit to whatever/whoever inspired me to write it. But in general, anything that made me inspired and that I needed to share with the women who followed me, is what I used to write my quotes!

I believe women are very powerful human beings! We have special intuition, we bear children inside our bodies and give them life! We take care of our kids, our partners, and we still find the time to take care of ourselves and our professional lives. Each woman does that in her own special way! No woman should compare herself to others! We are all unique, special, beautiful human beings! And we all have a lot to share in this world! Every single human being has a special gift they should share with the world! My biggest lesson in life so far is that we always have a choice to react to our dark emotions in a positive way. That can change our life path. It changed mine!

People will hurt you, people will make you feel jealous, people will ignore you, they will try to make you feel bad about yourself. And you will be mad, be angry, be upset, be jealous... but the reality is, as Eleanor Roosevelt said: "No one can make you feel inferior without your consent!". It is always our choice! And when someone hurts you, it's your own responsibility, not theirs', to fix your own hurt. It sounds easier said than done, right? But I assure you, that when you have positive thoughts, the positive energy in your body will speak louder and give you hope for a better outcome in the future! I truly believe that being happy is a matter of choice! Money and financial success will not bring anyone happiness, unless they have love in their lives, and if they are serving others in any way, shape or form...

I hope these quotes will bring you joy, a big smile on your face, or make you think deeply to have you transform your life to bring you fulfillment and happiness!

On this second edition, I added the last 6 months of motivational quotes I wrote on my Instagram account, after the first launch on April 2019. I also created my website during this time, so now you can learn more about me as well as the work I do with women at www.feelfabulousbyfabiana.com

# SELF-AWARENESS

*For any human being to be happy, feel fulfilled and satisfied in their own life, it can only happen if they learn about themselves, believe in who they are, accept who they are, and work on whatever part of themselves they believe is necessary to achieve that goal of being HAPPY! In the following pages are some quotes to give you inspiration to look deep inside yourself and become aware of who you are and how you can make changes for the better! Growing continuously and contributing your gift to the world is where the joy is!*

Creating awareness of the BAD HABITS we create ourselves is the key to breaking them! When you find yourself in that special moment of awareness, celebrate and break the bad habit once and for all. The strength that we have in our own minds to control our destiny is so powerful and a lot of us don't realize that. Become aware.... Good morning my friends! Let's have more of those breakthrough moments in our lives and eliminate all of our bad habits!

"You write your life story by the choices you make"! It's the power of intention that drives personal reality. So, let's intentionally write our stories, so that we are forever in love with it! And I would add for you to surround yourself with characters of that story that make it fulfilling and full of joy! Make the right choices! I say this to my daughter every single day! Life unfolds following all the choices we make... are you really writing your own life story the way you want it to unfold?

"Our perception holds the key to transformation". When your perception shifts, your personal story shifts! You have this power and have always had it! Let's try to change our perception from heaviness to lightness. Things become better because of YOU! Not because of externals...

We are never helpless! We have the power of our minds! Let's claim and use this power! Let's keep our self-confidence high, by believing and accepting who we really are! Let's embrace that and keep writing our beautiful life story.

FREEDOM! We cannot train ourselves to be free... we have to look inside and find our true selves, this is what will bring us the freedom that we want. Being free can mean different things to different people, but I still believe that when you are true to yourself, whatever freedom you are looking for, will be easier to find!

Let's remember that our days develop following our attitude for that day. If you are upset because it's a blizzard in the middle of April, you might be losing a chance to have a great snowy day with your friends/family or even by yourself, snuggled in a nice blanket by the fire reading that great book or a movie/show you have been meaning to read/watch! We have to remember that we should focus on what we can control, not what we can't. That way we don't get so frustrated, right? Choose to have a great snow day! I promise you that Spring will come! It always does!

Will Smith's words: FAIL EARLY, FAIL OFTEN, FAIL FORWARD! We should not have a negative relationship with failure... Failure is a massive part of being successful! So, let's get comfortable and actually seek failure in a way to learn the lessons that will drive us to be successful!

Be yourself, be fashionable, be happy! Expressing yourself through fashion is very powerful. But to each individual, it will only be powerful if it comes from within and is genuine. There is no such thing as being superficial because you like to dress up! You are expressing what's coming from inside. Don't let anyone tell you what to wear, unless you asked for their opinion and they took the time to understand what makes YOU feel fabulous! Again, take advantage of the people who inspire you to gather ideas on how to dress the way it makes you happy!

Let's act on our dreams and not only dream.... it's funny how we hear and say all the time "Dream big", "never stop dreaming", "follow your dreams", "chase your dreams" and so on... but the only way to make our dreams come true is by "waking up" and acting on them! Don't ever be afraid of making mistakes! You need to make them to learn how to do things better!

Life is not always about us, right? We have the tendency to take for granted people in our lives that are there for us every day, maybe because they are always doing things for us, what we expect them to do, but in reality, if they were not here tomorrow, our lives would not feel complete! Think about it and thank the people in your life you normally take for granted!

Do you feel there is something you would like to change in your life? If you keep on doing what you are doing, you will keep on getting what you get today. So, if you want change in your life, think about what attitudes or things you can change, to get what you want to get... we have one life! Don't allow your life to be turned into auto pilot mode... make it right for yourself and your loved ones!

Remember the story of the good and the bad wolf? The one we feed is the one who survives... Let's focus on feeding the good wolf inside of us, not the bad! If we focus all of our attention in everything negative that happens in our lives, we end up fooling ourselves that there is nothing good left! So, let's be smart and focus on feeding the positive traits we have inside of us!

"Being happy is a state of mind that is within each of us". Let's look inside and find that state of mind that triggers our happiness and follow that path every day! I believe that happiness is not a constant but comes in moments in our lives! Let's work towards having many of those moments, by understanding ourselves better. Remember that only YOU can make yourself happy! Other people and things will not make you happy. They might help you achieve that state of mind, but they are not the main character in your life to bring that feeling inside yourself!

There is no need to reinvent yourself after a break up of a long relationship! Dig deep inside and find who you've always been and also what made you happy during the relationship you've had. We become who we are from the experiences that we've had in life, right? So, what we can do is always look for what makes us feel happy, alive, excited about life and be that person! Trying to "reinvent" ourselves will never change the essence of who we are. Also, give yourself permission to process the pain of a relationship break up. The healing is different for each person, so take your time and go through your process in getting ready to move on, without outside pressure! Be it a boyfriend, a partner, a husband, every kind of break-up needs the right time to heal.

We all have strong negative feelings about certain things. When someone shares with you an idea, a comment or a suggestion that inspires fear, reluctance or disgust in you, try to approach it with curiosity and patience before you react! Your reaction to your strong feelings is what you should focus on. Who doesn't ever feel angry, envy, disgust, shame? We all do at certain points in our lives. The difference between each individual is how each one reacts to those strong negative feelings! Let's use our curiosity and patience to understand why we feel that way and try to have the best reaction to keep us sane, healthy and happy! You have a choice on how you will react!

We all have the chance to make the right choices in life! The choices that we make will determine what is going to happen in our future. If you believe you don't have any choices, talk to a friend, talk to someone who really loves you, and listen to what they have to say. The choices you have are maybe not exactly what you want at that moment, but you can build from there to achieve whatever your goal is. Let's try to make the right choices in life to write our story the way we want it to be written... We all have a choice!!

Bill Murray said: "Social Media is training us to compare our lives, instead of appreciating everything that we are. No wonder why everyone is depressed". I agree with parts of this statement. I believe we can and should appreciate and be inspired by other people's lives, making sure we don't forget to appreciate our own lives and if we are not happy with parts of it, make a change! It's healthy to be inspired by the right people... just make sure you understand the difference between being inspired, versus "aspiring" to other people's lives... Love who you are and change for the better what you believe you can!

We all create "lists" of things we want to do, goals we want to achieve, tasks we want to accomplish. But unfortunately, a lot of people end up not doing any of it or just a small piece. The easiest way to actually accomplish it is to create a real, attainable list and focus on it for at least 10-15 minutes a day! If you think you can't handle a long list, create a small one, get it done and then create a second one. That will take the pressure off your mind and make you feel like you actually can do it! And you CAN! Go for it now!

I heard Paul McCartney talking about how he came up with the song "Let It Be" and it inspired me to share it with you! He was dreaming that he was very worried about the future of his career and his mom, then already deceased, telling him "let it be, there will be an answer, let it be". And he woke up and wrote the song. It is so true that a lot of times on our moments of darkness, all we need is just to LET IT BE! Relax and let it be, and the answer will come! Once you know you have done all you can, LET IT BE!

"What are the things that can destroy a human being? Politics without principles, pleasure without commitment, wealth without work, wisdom without character, business without morality, science without humanity and prayer without charity." Gandhi. Be honest, be real, be yourself, and respect other people's feelings, ideas, and when you disagree with someone, please do that with grace! And when you realize that you are wrong, accept that, learn from it and move on...

Try to fulfill your souls with important things! My generation, the 40s, 50s and older, are really unique. We listened to our parents, our grandparents, our uncles and aunts. We also respected our teachers, the elderly, people we truly loved and that had more life experiences than us. We grew up playing outside, instead of spending hours in front of a screen. The songs we listened to had real meaning, bringing the best in us. Like the Beatles... they were not aggressive songs/raps, that bring up the rough side of people... I'd say we are a Limited edition that are less and less every day. The new generation might learn from us as to value what is important in life and what is good for our souls. Social media likes, without hard work doesn't fulfill anyone's soul... how do you fulfill your own soul?!

I am usually a very positive person! That helps me a lot to find happiness in certain things that might leave a negative person stressed out or unhappy. When things don't happen exactly how you expected, try to look at the situation with a positive attitude. For example, you planned a trip to a beautiful beach with your loved ones and when you get there it is raining nonstop. Instead of feeling that life is unfair and that you wasted time and money, try to enjoy the company and maybe get to know the place with different eyes! Our happiness is directly affected by our reaction/ attitude towards anything in life, really! Think about that and try to be positive looking for ways to have a different reaction to what is making you feel negative... you will even notice that people around you treat you nicer. Can you do that?

Could we get rid of the past? We simply can't! We never will... We are an ensemble of actions, omissions, desires, frustrations, thoughts and, forgetfulness of the past. We learn lessons from our past. We are also a whole set of possibilities that will define the path of our future! Therefore, "forget trying to forget" the past. Focus on making sure you have the future you really want, by focusing on your actions of the present! Are you present at this moment?

CHANGE is a big complex word, isn't it?! ... It's even more complex when it is directly connected to the changes we want to make in our own lives. If you want any change in your life, you have to understand that it requires expenditure of energy! Where attention goes, energy flows. A classic definition of CRAZY is to continue to do things the same way and expect different results! The truth is that if nothing changes, nothing changes!! It is that simple!! For new outcomes to give positive results on the outside, it might include the creation of something new on the inside. To achieve the results you want, you will very likely need to change attitudes or underlying beliefs. Are you ready for that?

Change actually happens in a moment! You might say "It took 5 years for me to make a change", but what you really find out is that change happens in a moment. It took you 5 years to get to the moment where you finally said: "Never again! I quit! Let's begin! I love you! It's over!" Our entire life changes in a moment... do you get that? You just need to believe you can change and if you need help to get to that breakthrough, go for it! Ask for help! You can make it!!

FREEDOM! This picture is from about 10 years ago when I lived in New York. Back when I didn't feel as much freedom as I do today, even though the picture looks like total freedom, doesn't it? Freedom seems to be desired by many people! But what exactly is freedom?! It could mean different things to different people! For me, being free means being able to be myself, to feel at ease with all parts of my life: from my love life, to professional, to financial and so on. If any of these areas are not making me feel at ease, if it makes me feel stuck, I don't feel freedom! That's when we need to understand the reasons why and work towards the desired solution, right?!

There is no such a thing as magic and you know it, right?! What really exists is hard work, being realistic and taking advantage of what is REAL in your life! Don't EVER feel sorry for yourself! Playing the victim doesn't help anyone! If you think about it, everything that happens in our adult lives, we DO have a say-in... we accept, we deny, we concur, we disagree, we cooperate, or we just sit there and let life take us places we never planned on going... Take control of your life! No blaming others... Think about all the future consequences of the actions and decisions

13

that you are making in your life today. Every single one of our actions will create a chain of reactions somewhere around us, and sometimes only inside ourselves alone... Be good and good comes back to you, be graceful even with the ones who are not graceful to you! This way, your life will be lighter and more rewarding!

Not all SUFFERING, not every PAIN enhances or strengthens people! Sometimes, for people who are not humble, suffering makes them lose their reasoning, they become bitter! The key to staying strong in the face of suffering is HUMILITY! I say this from personal experience! A person who is humble, knows she can't control everything, so she loses her desire for total control of the situation! That person is getting stronger! Be humble and you will become stronger and stronger!

Are you sabotaging your own personal goals?! When you are working on a plan to achieve some personal or professional goals, it's very important to take note and celebrate all that you're doing RIGHT in the process, all the small victories along the way! We tend to concentrate on what we want to change or what isn't working in our personal or professional lives, right? If you focus on making sure you celebrate every small victory, this will give you the confidence to keep you motivated to achieve that goal!

"CLARITY is POWER. Clarify what it is you really WANT at the level of your SOUL. The clearer you are about what you want - what you DESIRE - the easier it is to MAKE your VISION a REALITY!" Tony Robbins. If you are having a hard time clarifying what you really want, try listening to your gut! Remember the moments you felt bliss, felt accomplished. Visualize all the details involved in that situation and try to think about what careers would embrace those actions that created the good feelings in you! Tell me... what is your WANT? Have you found it?

The world we live in is the world we CHOOSE to live in, whether consciously or unconsciously! If we choose bliss, that is what we get! If we choose misery, we get that too! So, I guess the best thing for us to do, is to make sure we consciously choose the life we want to live! Don't let your life just pass by. Take charge of your own choices! And choose to be HAPPY!

What is PERSONAL FULFILLMENT? It includes positive things like joy, success, peace of mind, pleasure and recognition. But often, the most fulfilling things in life are the ones we've suffered for (one of the meanings of the word "passion" has to do with suffering), things we've sacrificed to attain (like training hard to play at a championship level), or things that are more about making others happy than they are about serving ourselves. In fact, the positive emotions of fulfillment tend to come most strongly as a result of hard work and sacrifice in service to an end that is bigger than just ME. Let's embrace suffering, find meaning in the pain, instead of just finding what is making you uncomfortable and removing it from your life. Understanding the pain, and working through it, will help you get closer to a fulfilling life.

HOPE requires ACTION! It's amazing to have hope and use that as a fuel to achieve your goals, but without action, your hopes will be just that... hopes. If you need inspiration, go look for it! Don't sit and wait for your hopes to become reality!! Do something about it! Remember that what inspires you, makes you who you are! Find the right inspiration that will get you to where you want to be!

JUDGING... Please don't judge because of difference of opinion. Actually, please don't judge at all...No one is better than you and you are no better than anyone! We are all individuals with our own qualities and flaws! Some people are humble enough to understand that as adults, we are the only ones who can make or break who we are as individuals... No one else has that power, even though it's easy to blame others! The world is full of hate and division. Let's start one by one changing that! I want the world to be different, but I can't change it by myself... Who is with me?!! Let's start by showing compassion and stop judging!

Don't be an IMMEDIATIST. It will only stress you, and you will give up on your plan. You may not have completed or reached a certain goal, because you have a very short-lived perspective on life! Think about it!! Take your time to plan, to understand what you really want, to look into yourself, and to follow YOUR time, not that of others!

KEEP YOUR HISTORY! I was at the Minnesota State Capitol today for a tour led by the architect who ran the recent remodeling of it. He talked about the importance of some art pieces that tell the real history of Minnesota. Even though a lot of people who would like to forget some of the stories, he reminded us that we cannot just erase our History. We can only learn from it, and never forget, so the bad things don't repeat themselves. I immediately thought about that in the context of our own life history! History has an important meaning. We shouldn't just erase it or delete it. We should keep it there, in the past, but always remember the lessons we learned from it! "You always have a choice! Choose to control your own attitudes and reactions to your dark feelings in a positive way. That can change your life path". This is how I live... my life has been really hard at times and knowing I DID have a choice of reacting to my emotions in a positive way, made a huge difference in my life path and in the lives around me! Be positive and make the choice that will take you to the path you really want!


Guess what?! YOU CAN DO THINGS DIFFERENTLY if you put your mind to it and also if you are open to see things with someone else's eyes. This serves for everything in life! A simple and very basic example for me was this weekend holiday trip. We had a day in Florida and a day in New York with events in both places, so in my mind the packing had to be my usual big suitcase with a couple of outfits to choose from. My husband asked me/ challenged me to pack everything in a carry-on! My first response was "No way..." then he talked about the efficiency of us arriving in NYC and not being late for our party because of a checked bag. Also unpacking and packing would be easier... I said I'd try. It took me a couple of days of considering what would fit in the carry-on, how could I be efficient taking only what I would actually wear and be OK with the fact that this was not my norm... I am proud to say I accomplished it! Not saying I will do it every time from now on... but I tried something different and it actually worked!


There are 60,000 voices in our heads talking to us every day! Some are useful and others are not useful at all, those are our Inner Critic and the useful ones are our Leader Within, with wisdom, love, compassion and no judgement! It's your choice to be aware and choose to listen to the Leader Within! This morning, I wanted to work out before my daily session, but my Inner Critic was not cooperating saying I was tired, and that I didn't have a lot of time. I chose to listen to my Leader Within who was telling me I could get in at least 20 minutes of workout and that I would feel great after! And I did!

When you live in a way that you honor your personal VALUES, that's when you get that amazing feeling of fulfillment in your life, right? Fulfillment is not something you can get or own. It is something you must live! How do you live by honoring your values? When you make any decisions in your life, make sure you align them with your top values! If family is your number one for example, make sure you think about that when deciding on anything that might impact your family negatively in the process. Most importantly, make sure you know clearly what your top values really are!! On your next big decision, try focusing on aligning it to your core values!!

The GREATEST ILLUSION we have as human beings is that we spend most of our time trying to control or change the outside world, so we will feel better on the inside. Guess what? That doesn't work! Fulfillment is so much more important! What makes us fulfilled is having a life with meaning! We must take time to figure out what it is! An easy way to start thinking about it is answering this question: What is the reason why you came to this world and what impact do you really want to have in other people's lives? Sounds corny, right? But that is a start!

The end of the year HOLIDAY SEASON can be an amazing time for some but can also be a very stressful time in other people's lives. I guess the pressure of thinking about all you have accomplished, or not, in the past year, plus thinking about what you want as goals for the new year, what changes you want to make for a better year, creates an uncomfortable feeling that I believe could be avoided! I constantly talk about the fact that we ALWAYS HAVE A CHOICE in our lives... You can choose to enjoy this season as a time to be with family and friends to celebrate the great energy and spirit the season brings. And you don't have to focus on your life like it's a business that needs to close the year with numbers and goals that need to be achieved by yearend! It's your life, not a business! Relax, and create your own timeframe of when you want things to happen, goals to be achieved, plans to be made... There is no need to have the mindset of: "New Year, new Me". You can always grow and evolve throughout the year, right? Don't pressure yourself to make a change "because" of the new year... Choose your own time! Make changes when you feel you are ready for them! Enjoy the season for what it should be: Family time! If you don't have family around, share that time with people you care about! HAPPY HOLIDAYS my friends!

I posted today my "BEST OF 2018" and after I posted all of the 60 pictures/videos, I realized how great my year was! It's interesting how we don't see clearly all the good things that we have in our lives! We have the tendency to focus on the hard, the complicated, the difficult... I will challenge you today, on the first of the year, to try and do your best to appreciate EVERYTHING you have good in your life and start looking at it with always a positive attitude. Would you accept this challenge? Maybe at the end of every month, go back and look at all the things you did that were good and special, and appreciate and cherish them! Let's start the new year with a POSITIVE attitude! Happy 2019!

You can BE HAPPIER by asking yourself QUALITY QUESTIONS instead of poor-quality ones. Think about it: if you ask yourself "What is wrong with me?" you will certainly come up with a lot of answers, right? Instead, ask yourself the quality questions that will bring you answers to improve your life. For example, "How can I get the quality love I really want in my life?" or "What do I really want in a close relationship or in my professional life?". Take time, even if it's only 10 minutes by yourself, with no interruptions to ask a quality question and think about the answer. You might not come up with one during those 10 minutes, but be assured that with time, the quality questions produce quality answers. They make you think deeper. Don't just ask and wait for an answer. Reflect on it, think hard, look deep inside for that HIGH-QUALITY ANSWER. If you love the questions you ask, then your life will become an answer to those questions! The better-quality questions you can ask about your life, the happier you will be!

WHY SOME SUCCEED WHILE OTHERS DON'T is a topic that has been explored by the greatest philosophers in history. The answer? Well, it is so surprisingly simple that perhaps this explains why it goes ignored by the masses: "A MAN'S LIFE IS WHAT HIS THOUGHTS MAKE OF IT" Marcus Aurelius. Success has nothing to do with formal education and even less to do with chronological age. Success is connected with the ability to believe- to believe that you can be, do, and have anything you set your mind to do. Just remember that success has many different connotations, depending on how you define it! Mother Teresa's definition of success was certainly different than Jeff Bezos... you get the point! Don't bend to others' definition of success. Don't feel pressured to follow the crowd. Build your own thoughts of how you want to be successful and go after it!

YOU WILL NEVER BE YOUNGER or more alive than you are right now! That means that if there is something you really want to do today, but you keep telling yourself you are too old for that, remember the above phrase! Of course, we have to be realistic. We might want to do/have or be somethings today but we are wise to recognize that our age is a true limitation, like getting pregnant after menopause... but for many other things, if it's just your mindset sabotaging your desire to do/be or have something because of your age, I suggest you shift your internal beliefs FROM: I'm too old now, TO: I am the perfect age, FROM: It's too late now, TO: There is plenty of time, FROM: I can't, TO: Of course I can! You can shift your mindset and the perception of your current reality by taking the time to do internal work!

What is an EXTRAORDINARY LIFE for you? It's what you think it should be!! It is important to know that nothing is inherently good or bad; rather, it simply is. What shapes your reality is your perception - how you choose to view the situation and whether you choose to put a positive or a negative moniker on it. So, find the positive perspective of your life and go live your extraordinary life!

Getting into balance is so desirable! But WHAT DOES BALANCE MEAN? It actually means leaving NOTHING out! We all have parts of ourselves, something about our bodies or our personality that we are not proud of. The natural tendency is to ignore perceived weaknesses and flaws. But self-care isn't about denial or rejection. It's about inclusion. Everything about you is included in the light of kindness and support. Going to the very source of your mind, is what will give you the ability to silently rebalance your entire system. Yet we can help this process along by making certain positive lifestyle changes. We have all learned the need for proper diet, regular exercise, stress management and so on. The REAL PROBLEM ISN'T NOT KNOWING, IT'S NON-COMPLIANCE. Our massive tendency is to NOT do what we know is good for us. The way around non-compliance isn't to force yourself to be good. IT DOESN'T WORK! Because the urges you push down will always return. The best motivation is inspiration. The most inspiration you can offer yourself is self-compassion: nurture your personal growth! Look for inspiration to improve your inner self! Be kind to yourself and balance will happen!

A lot of us have been taught from an early age to suppress our EMOTIONS. We get messages like: "Don't be a baby". "Be a big girl OR big boy". Unfortunately, when we turn down the volume in our emotional experience, we also turn down the volume on our aliveness and authenticity as well. EMOTIONS ARE ENERGY and when they are flowing freely, they bring us tremendous energy and provide the fuel for us to transform and grow! However, when we are not willing or able to allow our emotions to flow freely, that energy can get stuck in our bodies and can create all kinds of physical issues and disease. Instead of being concerned that your emotions will take over and run the show, think that you should allow yourself to be present and experience whatever you are feeling. The energy of the emotions will move naturally and will become a resource that we can harness to create powerful, positive change in our lives. That can be your choice!

YOUR PROBLEM IS YOUR GIFT! Our problems make us grow, sculpt our soul and get us ready to become a better version of ourselves! Naïve is the one who believes that a life without problems is a perfect life! Someone who doesn't experience any hardships, will end up crumbling when that happens... Going through a problem, understanding where it's coming from, looking for a solution and ultimately resolving it is what creates the life experiences that will shape us to become a better human. But that will only happen IF you make an effort to learn from every hardship you go through. But if you focus on being the victim, on holding on to that grudge because of a problem you've had in your life, unfortunately you will not grow with that experience! You will become a bitter human being, and bitterness attracts bitterness. Kindness attracts kindness! If you are going through a hardship at this moment, I would like to send you a lot of good vibes to help you find your way out of that problem and learn a lot from it! Remember that every problem has a solution! EVERY SINGLE ONE! Maybe not exactly what you expected, but there is always a way out!

"Imagine what would happen if each one of us knew ourselves as fully and deeply as possible. And that we led each day of our lives consciously and compassionately, without projecting our

23

emotions onto others, or allowing our egos to distort reality. If everyone did whatever work was necessary to get to know themselves better and took responsibility for being the best self he or she could be, I believe the world would be a different place, a better place." Gisele Bündchen. This is exactly how I feel today in the stage of my life I am living now! What do you say if I challenge you to try to know yourself fully and deeply to create a better world? We all have amazing gifts inside ourselves, but we need to be curious to find them, when we are not aware of them!


BEING SMART DOESN'T KEEP YOU FROM DOING DUMB THINGS! The trick is to be aware and realize/accept the things you are not good at, and not waste your time and energy in that place! Learn from the mistakes and move on. It's worth it to do something you are not good at if your intention is to enjoy or master it. But staying in that place of "incompetence" with no valid reason is NOT SMART... for example: if you are a smart professional but not good at tech stuff, don't waste your time fixing your PC at home to save some bucks or because you want to prove to yourself you can do it! Pay someone who can do it efficiently and make better use of the time you would have "wasted" trying to fix the PC while being frustrated. It's OK to do those dumb things once, but more would actually be dumb!


JUST BECAUSE YOU ARE OFFENDED DOESN'T MEAN THAT YOU ARE RIGHT... We have our own way of seeing/interpreting/understanding situations in life. Your truth might not be someone else's truth. I believe that respectful arguments are healthy, not imposing our own opinion onto others. When I feel offended by someone's truth, first I assess if it's worth my time and energy to bring a respectful argument to express how I feel AND why. How would that affect my life... If I don't feel it is worth it, I just let it go and respect that we think differently and move on. It's always good to remember that

24

people's individual life experiences are their own and that is what creates their truth.

"Let's get rid of the Rear-View Syndrome" Italo Marsili. We should focus on moving from NOW ON FORWARD, and not look back all the time! We need to look back maybe 5% of the time to make sure we move forward nicely and smoothly, learning from our past mistakes. Our cars have a big front window, so that we look forward most of the time and a small rear mirror, for us to look back just a few times while we drive. In our lives it's the same. We should be looking at the NOW ON FORWARD and stop looking at our back history all the time.

There is a big pressure for CONFORMITY nowadays. They talk about a formula, and if you can just get this formula right, you will be great. Reality is more often than not that the people who achieve real greatness don't fit the formula at all. In fact, they break the formula and do something completely different. You have to be creative and step out of your boundaries a little bit. The greatest people are driven, focused, dedicated and they just LOVE what they do! Do you want to be GREAT at what you do? Find what you love, be driven, focused, dedicated and you can achieve greatness!

WE CREATE OUR OWN LIMITATIONS. DON'T BE YOUR WORST ENEMY! CONTROL YOUR OWN THOUGHTS. I'm sure you've heard this many times: "we are our worst enemies". What I guess that means, is that we are the only ones who can create the feeling of insecurity of feeling small, being negative, creating obstacles. It comes from our own minds, our own thoughts triggered by our environment and people around us, but we are the ones who create the emotion through our own thoughts. So, when you are feeling down, or feeling like you want to quit what you KNOW in your heart you can succeed, take a couple of minutes... breathe and consider all the details of your thoughts. What is reality and what is just your fear of what's about to come or what is NOT coming? You can thrive by persisting, once your gut tells you that what you are doing is the right thing to do! Don't let your fears break your dreams! Fight your fears, allow your inner wisdom to take over. Listen to your True Self, to your GUT. Being realistic and knowing that something isn't feasible is OK. You will learn how to deal with that, by looking for alternative solutions. But acting out of fear, is just going to destroy your own dreams! Don't let that happen! Take control of your own thoughts!

CHANGE COMES FROM ACCEPTANCE, NOT FROM RESISTANCE! It's easy to complain about our problems and blame others to take away our own responsibility for the changes we want in our own lives. You will not have any positive change in your life if you don't accept the problem/situation that you are facing. When you are complaining or blaming, or staying in that victim mode, you are resisting the acceptance of the situation. Once you accept that you cannot continue doing what you are doing and realize that ONLY YOU can act on it, is when change happens! No one will change your life for you. YOU WILL! What are you doing today to start accepting your unwanted situation and take action to make changes?

REASON identifies your needs, establishes your objectives, how you will resolve your problems. But your EMOTIONS are the fuel that will make you move forward! So next time you are feeling a strong emotion, ask yourself: "Something has created that feeling in me, what has created this emotion I am feeling? What is this something?" When you find the answers, use that emotion as a fuel to accomplish something good for yourself and your loved ones. Sometimes, even the strongest of the hard feelings, can be a fuel for you to achieve something good in your life!

"When we have a regret, we normally say "I wish I knew better then". The reality is that we DO know better now, and we would NOT know better today if this regret didn't exist..." Fabiana Peterson

OUR OPINION CAN CHANGE DRASTICALLY ABOUT AN ISSUE OR SITUATION WHEN WE ACTUALLY EXPERIENCE IT! Think about this: how many times in your life have you formed an opinion about something but when you see yourself IN that situation, your opinion drastically changes? And that doesn't mean your opinion is wrong! You just have a different truth. A couple of simple and obvious examples are divorce and having kids. My opinion about both changed drastically once I was actually experiencing them. And both happened decades after I was born, which means I had years of formed opinions that changed, but never changed as drastically as they did when I lived those situations. The message I would like to share is that we should always be careful when giving our opinion without having lived the situation as well as being respectful to opinions that are different than yours. Everyone's truth and life experiences are different.

"GRATITUDE changes your relationship with life from an attitude of rejecting and defending, to one of acceptance and appreciation. Research has shown that this shift involves emotions, beliefs and even our bodies. Because gratitude has a positive effect even in ourselves, it becomes an ENGINE FOR HOLISTIC CHANGE." Deepak Chopra. These changes begin inside of us. When you feel your energy shifting because of a negative thought, try to think about the things you are grateful for, maybe even something related to that specific thought! For example: if you are mad at your mother, first thing you can do is think about the things related to her that you are grateful for. That will immediately shift your energy and you will look at your negative thoughts with a different perspective! Isn't it true that 2 people could be looking at the same situation, having the same background, but their perception could be totally different? Try to find that positive side in you, where you can see the good even on the worst things are happening in your life. I assure you it works, because I try that every time. It won't immediately take away your negative thoughts, but it will shift your energy and that is a start!

Who inspires you? Why do they inspire you? I assume because you look up to them, right? My question is: what is holding you back to do what is inspiring you in the first place? It's great to be inspired by others to do and be someone better, but you need ACTION for anything to change in your life! That old saying: if you keep doing what you are doing you will keep getting what you get! Let's change that! Start TODAY acting towards what inspires you!

We are ALL Instagram influencers... Think about it... it doesn't matter if you have a couple of followers or a million followers, in both cases, you DO have the power to influence whoever is following you, right? To a different scale in each case, but you still DO! This is an amazing way to share the right message, make a difference, positively influence other people's lives! If you really care, and do it with your heart, your message will be captured, and hopefully make a difference!

"When I have no judgement, I see everyone with kindness. Compassion can change your world! And there is a link between gratitude and compassion" Deepak Chopra. When you have kindness in your heart, you are being compassionate. But sometimes it feels impossible to feel compassionate when we feel judgmental towards someone we believe is doing/acting wrong. There is an ego problem of righteousness on being judgmental... A good technique to escape this is to try and be thankful for that person, adopting the attitude of that person's parent, who doesn't judge, just try to be compassionate and helpful! And once we stop judging others, we stop judging ourselves!!! I uploaded a video that explains this in detail on my YouTube channel.

Let's keep an eye on the stories we tell ourselves over and over again. Which ones serve us, and which ones don't... I finished reading the book Inheritance from Dani Shapiro, where she tells her story about finding out at 55 years old, after a DNA test, that her father was not her father... the way she develops the narratives is super interesting. But what caught my attention was her struggle to hold on to a story and keep it real for her. We tend to tell ourselves stories throughout our lives that sometimes help us move forward but other times, certain stories, holds us back or make it really hard to move forward. Take a look at the stories you are telling yourself and rewrite the ones that don't serve you well!

If you notice that you are overriding your own morals and values to achieve certain goals personally and professionally, that's the time you have to stop and rethink your strategy... what are you doing this for? Or WHO are you doing this for? If the answer actually doesn't bring you back to what you truly value, it's certainly time to make changes, because soon enough you will have negative results in your personal and professional lives... Have you had that experience before? I guess that sometimes we might do it without even noticing.... that's where our self-awareness plays a big role!

What makes a person a person?
We have a certain perception of who we are, but if we are not real and authentic, the perception others will have about us might be totally different than our reality! Why not do a test? Ask 3 different people not directly connected to each other, but all close to you, what they think about you and compare notes! That could be a very interesting exercise!

LIFE IS PRECIOUS! You are precious! Appreciate your health, your warm bed, your food on the table, your ability to walk, talk, and all the things and people we normally take for granted in our lives... instead of focusing on what is wrong with your life, focus on what you can appreciate every single day! I promise you that by doing that, you will bring a different kind of energy throughout your day, and when we see things with positive eyes, positive things happen!

Are we too busy worrying to notice the "miracles" in our lives? Unfortunately, we have the tendency to be scared and focused on the bad things more than we appreciate and enjoy the good things in life! That creates unnecessary worry and anxiety in our lives! We actually end up missing some "miracles" that might happen, because we don't have our focus in the right place!
Let's start focusing our attention on all of the good things and also what really matters in our lives. What miracle you might have missed in the last few days, weeks or months? Look back and you might find one

"Dreams don't work unless you do!" John C. Maxwell. How hard are you working to reach your own dreams? This message resonated with me today while I was working on a Workshop to help divorced women to feel fabulous about themselves after their divorce. After we get divorced, our dreams don't end...

they just change! And we should never forget that for dreams to come true, there is a need for ACTION! And I truly believe that for a woman who suffered through divorce, doing inner work to feel good about herself again is key to help her reach her new dreams! If you have just gotten divorced, what are you doing to take care and feel good about yourself?

Nature is strong and amazing and so are you! Therefore, stop lying to yourself! "I'll start tomorrow...", or "I'll do it tomorrow..." Why wait until tomorrow if you can start making changes today? Think about what is really holding you back! Most of the time is fear, convenience or pure laziness! Start by making the changes, doing what you want to do, take action today, start now! Your future is in your hands, no one else's!

"THERE IS POWER IN OUR ACTIONS! EXERCISE YOUR ABILITY TO CHOOSE OR JUST TAKE A BACK SEAT AND WATCH YOUR OWN LIFE GO BY..." These were words of a High School graduate during their graduation event. She was spot on! You have total control of your own actions. Not of the environment around you, but you DO have a choice to say yes or no to everything that happens in your life. You should feel empowered that you DO have a say about where your life is going next. It might not be necessarily where you first expected it to go, but considering all circumstances around you, bear in mind you ALWAYS have a choice. CHOOSE WISELY and make sure you do choose and not just let things happen without your consent

HOW DO YOU KNOW IF YOU ARE SUCCESSFUL? It is such a personal understanding of what exactly success means to you, isn't it? Maybe in your head you feel that you are not successful, when in the mind of certain people, who certainly see the world differently than you, they see that you are for sure a successful person! In that case, you might listen and end up agreeing with that person. But the other way around... not so much! If you think you are successful, but someone around you doesn't agree, our first reaction is to think that person is jealous! Well, think twice from now on... maybe they just see the world differently than you and their understanding of what success means, doesn't match yours. Well, what is the message here?! Stick to what YOU understand success is, since it's your own life, and go for it, so that YOU feel accomplished in your own way!

"I WANT TO BE A HEALER IN THIS HURTFUL WORLD. I WANT TO MAKE A DIFFERENCE IN PEOPLE'S LIVES!" I heard this today from the Minister who was giving a eulogy of a friend. And this made me think about a question I am now going to pose to you: WHAT DO YOU WANT TO BE SAID IN YOUR OWN EULOGY SOME DAY? hopefully many, many years from now. I want to be remembered by how I made people feel when they were around me, by the positive impact I've made in their lives. THAT hopefully will be my legacy! Not about material things I've had or things I've accomplished, but by genuinely living in everyone's hearts who were touched by me.

JUDGEMENT versus OPINION. In our heads, when we feel that someone is judging us, we associate the word judgement with shame. It makes us feel bad for being judged. But if you remember that person is actually just saying "their opinion" about you (which it is!) that on its own turns the feeling of shame, into your personal choice to accept or not.

JOY IS WHAT WE SHOULD FOCUS ON... NOT HAPPINESS! I heard this 10 min video from Matthew McConaughey and it was so clear to me that our quest for "happiness" can just end up frustrating us. Let's focus on finding joy in all that we do! Make the choices in life that will get you there, this way, "happiness" will be a consequence of all the joy you have created in your life! "Happiness to men is a certain outcome. It's results reliant! If happiness is what you are after, you're gonna be let down frequently and you're gonna be unhappy most of the time! But JOY is not a choice, it's not a response to some result. It's a constant. Joy is the feeling from doing what we are fashioned to do, no matter the outcome...." Matthew McConaughey

"Even some rocks, the densest of all forms, undergo a change in their molecular structure, turn into crystals and so become transparent to the light." Eckhart Tolle. We can and should change! We should be constantly evolving, doing inner work to bring our best true self to the world! What are you doing today to improve your life in ways that you can actually transform yourself into the best version you can ever be?

DO YOU BELIEVE IN THE LAW OF ATTRACTION?! I TOTALLY DO! Whatever way you act in life, comes back to you! It's not magic! It is just logic. If you are a negative person, that is what you will get back in your life. Not because of anyone, but only because of you! The way you see things: if it's always with a negative connotation, negative eyes, etc. You will be living in that negative perspective! If you are a positive person, that is also what you will get back. It doesn't mean that you will ONLY have positivity, but when negative things happen, being positive, using positive energy, looking from a positive perspective, it will help you deal with the negative situation in a way that won't have bad lasting effects! See?! It's not magic! You have a choice on how you want your life to unfold! Start looking at things from the bright side, from a positive perspective! Tag someone you believe would be curious about this and maybe start changing their perspective!

EMOTIONAL INTELLIGENCE: It's the capacity to be aware of, control and express your emotions, and to handle interpersonal relationships with no judgement and with empathy. Taking responsibility for how you are feeling is the first step to emotional intelligence. No blaming others. They might have brought your feelings to the surface, but they are your feelings and your responsibility alone to deal with it!

WHEN YOU ARE HURTING, LET THAT FEELING RUN THROUGH YOU! Allowing yourself to feel the pain, cry, talk about it or write about it. But let it run in your body! That is a good way to release it, instead of allowing it to fester inside you. That can cause you to get physically sick! Let the pain leave your heart. This is a great way to start healing from it.

HOW DO YOU MAKE FRIENDS WITH YOUR INNER CRITIC? We all know well enough that we have a negative and a positive voice talking to us in our heads all the time. Unfortunately, our negative voice, the "Inner Critic", talks to us more often than the positive one. The first thing we can do is to become aware when that is happening. It's actually not very hard. The negative voice always shows up when we feel fear, insecurity, careful and many other feelings that can show the "Inner Critic" as being a "protector" for us, or in many cases, our own "saboteur", sabotaging our own attitudes that end up bringing us to failure. But if we choose to listen to our positive voice, our "True Self or Leader Within" we have a way better chance to succeed. When I say making friends, I mean, listening to your negative voice to make sure it is really not a self-protection method. If it's clear it's sabotaging you, ask your "True Self" what your own heart would say in that situation. The answer might surprise you! Make an effort to listen to your positive voice, you "True Self" instead of your Inner Critic.

LET'S BE CONSCIOUSLY AWARE OF THE CHOICES WE MAKE EVERY MOMENT! I always talk about the fact that we always have a choice to act in ways that affect our life path positively. As Deepak Chopra said, we have unconscious choices in life, that are conditioned by our life experiences. But we don't have to make those choices unconsciously. For example, when someone insults you, you unconsciously feel insulted, because you are conditioned to do so. But the reality is that you have the choice to NOT feel insulted by whatever they said, principally if you know what they are saying is not valid. Life is a continuum of choices, conscious and unconscious. I am asking you to listen to your heart, your gut, before you make a choice. Be conscious about that choice. Your body will tell you which choice is the best one for you, and the ones around you that will be affected by the actions you decide to take. Also, where your life is right now, is a consequence of all the actions you have taken so far, therefore, please don't blame or complain about it. Take control of your choices from now on! Become aware and make conscious choices!


CHANGE COMES FROM ACCEPTANCE, NOT FROM RESISTANCE! It's easy to complain about our problems and blame others to take away our own responsibility for the changes we want in our own lives. You will not have any positive change in your life if you don't accept the problem/situation that you are facing. When you are complaining or blaming, or staying in that victim mode, you are resisting the acceptance of the situation. Once you accept you cannot continue doing what you are doing, you create the awareness and realize that you, ONLY YOU need to act on it, is when change happens! No one will change your life for you. YOU WILL! What are you doing today to start accepting your unwanted situation and take action to make changes?

# Moment of reflection! What can you improve regarding your self-awareness?

_____

_____

_____

_____

_____

_____

_____

_____

_____

_____

_____

_____

_____

_____

_____

_____

_____

_____

# SELF-LOVE

*We can only feel confident, strong and ready to face any challenges in life, if we love ourselves. If we are kind to ourselves. Loving ourselves is a key element to being loved by others. In the next pages you will read words that will hopefully make you reflect about the importance of self-love. If you are living your life honoring your values, respecting everyone around you and sharing your gift with the world, I have no doubt that you are amazing! Don't let anyone tell you differently.*

Let's switch the Happiness button in our brains to have a magical day! Let's love ourselves unconditionally, because it's essential to our happiness! Let's love the person that we are. We do NOT need other's approval to love ourselves fully! Let's give wherever we go, even if it's just a smile or a compliment!

I like this passage from Arianna Huffington's book: "Let's play the game of life in a way that will make us feel truly fulfilled. Let's make sure that we are valuing the right things and the right people that will bring us a fulfilling life!" Let's make ourselves proud! Let's be brave and believe in ourselves by doing the right things for us and for our loved ones! When we start focusing on ourselves from within and working our own issues, life makes more sense and the feeling of fulfillment kicks in!

Feeling fabulous comes from within!! A beautiful dress and great accessories will not make you feel fabulous overall if you are not happy with who you are! I mean happy inside! But while you are working towards the goal of feeling fabulous, it helps a lot to focus on the positives in your life! I always do that, and it works!! Everyone has something positive in their lives, I assure you that YOU DO! Sometimes we just take for granted the little things, but if we focus on them, they will give us the strength to move forward towards our goal of being happy overall, feeling fabulous!

If we don't love ourselves truly for who we are, we will not have a partner who will truly love us for who we really are! So, let's keep working with our inner self to make sure we are happy and love who we truly are!

Being vulnerable is NOT a weakness! Got this text from Brené Brown and loved it! "When we hear the word vulnerability, often we associate it with fear, shame and weakness! Vulnerability is a direct path to self-love and self-worth! When you allow your true self to be seen, you are telling yourself that you are worthy, beautiful and deserving of love!" Let's open up ourselves to be vulnerable!

Turning 47 today and feeling fabulous! I do my best to accept aging as it comes, but I refuse to give in to age! I work hard to keep my body healthy and my mind young, so that I can age in a healthy and happy way! Age is just a number! Let's accept and embrace our reality in the best way possible! Let's age gracefully....

How can we feel confident?! In reality, no one can give us confidence... confidence comes from within. Comes from being happy with who we are and accept what was given to us when we came to this world! We can always work to improve what we believe would make us more complete, but our essence never changes!! Look inside and find your happy self, accept who you are, change just what makes you feel complete, that last bit to bring you your full confidence! Nothing is more beautiful than a person who loves themselves the way they are, keeping their morals and their values and respecting others! That is so important! You will never be complete and confident and fulfilled by putting someone else down! Let's look inside ourselves and find that confidence that is right there!

We shouldn't be comparing ourselves to others. We are 'individuals' for a reason. We are all unique and special in our own way! Every single person has their own gifts. Being competitive is very healthy, because it brings in us the eagerness to be better! But what we should focus on is the wish to be better than WE were before. Let's stop comparing ourselves to other people! Each individual is different physically, mentally, life experiences, etc.! When you start comparing yourself or your life with someone else's, try to focus on YOU, and YOU alone. Compare only what you were yesterday to what you are today and what you want to be tomorrow!

Age is just a number! Really!! I am 47, and believe I have the wisdom of my age, but I feel way younger in spirit! Our bodies of course start showing the signs of age, but with a healthy diet and exercising often, you can keep being healthy for many, many years! Another very important thing that keeps us young, is love and friendship! If you love and feel loved by people that are close to you, that will keep you young at heart!

Editing a picture to post in social media is something a lot of people do nowadays, because it's easy with the technology available out there. But what people don't realize is that they are not being truthful to themselves and to others, when you airbrush and edit a picture to fix something you don't like about your appearance. That is not a good thing. If there is something you would like to improve about your skin, or your body, you can try to do real life work on it, but don't lie to yourself. An edited picture is not going to change your reality. Accept who you are, love your body the way it is, and if you want to make any healthy changes, go for it, realizing that beauty is not a standard! You will feel beautiful if you love yourself, and that will make it easier for others to love you and see your own beauty as well!

I love this picture! First because it was my amazing sister who took it and to whom I was smiling! But also, because it captures clearly who I am with the wrinkles around my eyes and forehead, because of my age, and the imperfections of my skin! But for me, it also shows this Brazilian's love for life, family, friends, fitness and a healthy lifestyle! So, I decided to post this picture to say that we have to remember that our physical appearance is simply one aspect of us!! True beauty lies beneath the surface and is made up of a composite of our mental attitude, our actions, and the way we impact other people's lives. Let's embrace our uniqueness!! We don't need to use any Apps to "fix" anything on our pictures! Choose the right light and the right pose that will give you a result that will show who you really are! Of course, you have to feel good about it! Light is everything on a picture, I have to admit!! I will be very direct here: there is no need to lie to yourself and others, right?! Let's have the courage to live a life that is faithful/truthful to who we really are! You can achieve this truth/faith, first of all, by assuming a deadly serious commitment to NOT lie to yourself and others. Kill the lies from now on! Choose the right light to show how beautiful you really are!

This picture proves to me that there is light at the end of the tunnel. If you have the right attitude, actions and reactions and make the right decisions during your times of suffering, you become stronger. Happiness is a consequence of the actions you end up taking! I've been happily married to the love of my life for over a year now after some suffering that could have turned my life the other way. I say this because we have to understand that not every suffering, not every pain can improve or strengthen people! Sometimes, for people that are not humble, the suffering can make them go crazy or become bitter and self-absorbed people! I believe that the key to become strong in the face of suffering is HUMILITY!! Someone who is humble, knows that they cannot control everything, therefore they lose this fetish of total control, of absolute dominance. And this person will become stronger and stronger! Have you looked inside yourself lately and seen what you really want to see?!

Why some people worry so much about what others say about them?! If you know you are following your personal morals and values, and you are totally respecting everything and everyone around you, you should not care about things that others say that makes you feel bad. Of course, we should listen to what others have to say, because it might bring up something you haven't noticed before. You can always ignore the haters. Those so unhappy with themselves that they need to go out and try to make others feel bad to feel better about themselves. And always make sure to listen to the ones you know have your best interest in their hearts! No one is perfect, but if you surround yourself with people who are worth your time, love and attention, their opinion towards you should matter, but you should still not worry... YOU ARE WHO YOU ARE because of the choices you make! If you don't like something about yourself, do something! Choose to be better! Do you like who you really are?!

Be true to yourself! By being just who you really are, people will respect you a lot more. The problem is that people are insecure by nature. They have not experienced the truthfulness that leads to true freedom. A person can only form a real truthful personality that is robust and mature, if her choices are made in an environment of freedom! The actions in our lives that are built on the basis of lies and falsehood, have no consistency, they will not last! And knowing they will not last, we get anxious. We are going to become really sad. So many anxieties, lethargies, hopelessness, and a lot of meaninglessness that people are experiencing out there happens because they were building a life on the basis of lies. On the basis of falsehood. Be who you really are! Have you ever thought about that?!

"No one can make you inferior without your consent". Eleanor Roosevelt. Don't allow anyone to make you feel bad about yourself! The only person that can be your measure about how you are doing in life is you! Only you! You surely will be smart to listen to the opinion of the ones whom you know have your best interest at heart, but the decision to feel bad about yourself has to come from you, knowing that you need to improve on certain areas of your life! Are you feeling bad about something in your life? If that's the case, do something about it! Don't let that feeling drag you down! Always remember that no one is perfect, and change is always possible!!

How can you actually feel EMPOWERED?! It can be different for each person. For us women, it could be as simple as wearing an outfit that makes us feel pretty, empowering our femininity! It could be a mother feeling that their teen child actually listens to her and asks for advice! Or it could be at work, where you feel you are ready to run that meeting where you totally command the topic! In any case, feeling empowered is directly connected to how you feel about yourself, and how people around you add to that equation with their attitudes towards you! So, if you want to feel empowered, work hard on yourself to feel good about who you are and surround yourself with quality people that make you feel fabulous about yourself with their positive energy and honest support!

SELF-LOVE, SELF-IMAGE and SELF-AWARENESS come hand in hand with your FITNESS journey! We are all different, unique and special in our own way! There is not one woman whose body looks exactly like another, right? So why bother comparing yourself to anyone but yourself yesterday and how you want to look tomorrow?! I feel inspired by the ones that have focus, dedication and commitment to achieve their fitness goals, and that gives me some of the motivation needed to reach my own goals!! But remember again: YOU ARE UNIQUE! You should always aim for the best that YOU can be! Not "look like" someone else, don't you agree?!

Every human being is naturally resourceful, creative and whole! Therefore, you are too! If you are feeling unhappy with your fitness journey, or the way you look, you can make a choice to make a change in your lifestyle to get closer to your goals! You ALWAYS have a choice! Remember that the only thing we can control in our lives is our actions, reactions and attitudes towards the feelings and emotions that we have. We can't control the feeling itself, or the situations happening around us, but we have a choice to react to those in a positive way. Same regarding any comments from people around you that put you down. You can't control what people say, and you also cannot control how you feel about those comments. But you have a CHOICE and the CONTROL of how you will react to those comments, right? Tame your Inner Critic! We all have one inside of us...You can't control your exact weight or how your body naturally looks, but you have a choice and can control your attitude towards that situation, which is working out and eating healthy. Once you realize that we DO have the CHOICE of how we will react to everything that happens in our lives, it will start to become clearer. A healthy lifestyle is good for anyone. Surround yourself with people that bring out the best in you and share good energy, seems way too simple, but it helps a lot on your fitness journey!

Being at PEACE does not mean to be in a place where there is no noise, trouble or hard work. It means to be in the midst of those things and still be calm in your heart! And INNER PEACE begins the moment you choose NOT to allow another person or event to control the reactions to the emotions they create in you. You take the lead and control your reactions! That will give you inner peace!

CRITICS - don't worry about the feedback/opinion of the critics who have never done or been in your situation. Listen to the ones who lived it, who did it! Or the ones who are trying hard to put themselves in your shoes. Those people will be able to give you valuable feedback.

PITY should be kept in your hall of feelings towards others, NOT YOURSELF! Some people say that feeling sorry for someone else is to diminish that person. That is not a true statement! We only have control over our own actions, so we have no reason to feel sorry for ourselves, because we have a choice to do things the way we want, and if we mess up, it's our own fault and we are the only ones who can fix it! But when we watch someone else acting in a way that harms us or others, and knowing that person can't see what they are doing even after we try to explain, there is nothing else we can do but feel sorry for them and pray they find a way to control their actions in a better way... I consider having pity as an act of compassion towards someone else... don't you agree?

TRUE LOVE is an act of free benevolence! You feel true love towards someone else when all that you want is just to see that person happy. The selfish YOU disappears and you give yourself completely into that beautiful and genuine feeling! True love can only happen when you know who you really are, and you love yourself the way you are. When that happens, your heart has the space and the maturity to mold and feel selfless love for someone else. If you are not happy with who you are, you won't have space to have that selfless feeling for someone else... Start appreciating who you are, love yourself! If there is something you don't love, think about how you can change it, improve it or make it better! No one is perfect, so accept the limitations you have that are not holding you back regarding your Life purpose!

BEING STRONG! What does that really mean? Honestly, it might mean different things for different people in different life situations, right? The reality is that each one of us CAN CHOOSE what strong means to us! As adults we can always choose anything about our own lives! In practical terms, I do my Upper Body workout with no more than 15 or 20lbs, and I feel super strong! I raised my daughter for about 5 years almost alone when her dad was living in Africa: I felt really strong! I chose to be strong! I had a very hard to deal with boss once and I chose to be strong everyday going to work! It's our choice! It's our mindset! CHOSE TO BE STRONG AND YOU WILL BE!

If you want to BECOME THE BEST VERSION OF YOURSELF, you must start today to build up your own self-talk. In order to truly grow, you must dare to move out of your comfort zone with respect to your own thought process. Find different perspectives! You have infinite potential inside of you. You are not here by accident. If there is a burning desire you hold in your heart, know that it can be attained! You simply need to embed into your subconscious the belief you can do and achieve what you want to achieve. "It's not who you are that holds you back, it's who you think you are not." Denis Waitley

HOW TO CREATE POSITIVE CHANGE in yourself? That seems to be a hard question, but it is so simple! You have to discover your inner source of strength, your sense of purpose that empowers you, energizes you and animates you! When you tap into this deeper meaning in your life and purpose, everything changes! You amplify your ability to understand yourself, to understand others, to create value for others! When you create value for others, you'll be creating more value for yourself as well!

SHARE YOUR GIFT! The world will thank you! I loved a post today by a coach in California! It talks about us nowadays "hiding" our gifts because we don't want to show off, it's not nice, because we have to be humble. Really? When you have a gift, a talent, something that is coming from your heart, from a place of love, you better share it! Be proud of yourself! Don't hide it! Every human being has a gift! You just need to find out what it is! It could be just that you always make people smile, or in the case of my daughter, her voice touches people's hearts when she sings opera! It doesn't matter what it is, but if it is coming from your heart, from a place of love and if it will impact, inspire and make a difference in other people's lives: SHARE IT!! But listen... I am not telling you to be a "Beech" As I said, if you are doing it from your heart and with a positive outlook on the outcome for you and for others, GO FOR IT! Sing, dance, speak up, share your wisdom, your gift and inspire others!


SELF-LOVE! It's interesting I chose to talk about self-love in Valentine's week, right? The reality is that TO FIND REAL LOVE in a relationship, you have to FIRST LOVE and RESPECT YOURSELF! There is no secret for a relationship to work! If you love and respect yourself AND have the same level of respect for your partner, honoring your values and theirs through your attitudes, your relationship should flow naturally! Transparency and communication are also essential! I hope you have a great Valentine's day tomorrow and if you have no partner at this time, go out to celebrate yourself! Your love for who you are, the way you are! When we love ourselves, our light shines brighter!


FORGIVING YOURSELF is key in allowing you to move forward! Forgive yourself for not meeting your own impossible standards and understanding that you are worthy. Be kind to yourself when you are not able to reach a specific goal or when it's clear you made a mistake! Maybe you didn't create a realistic goal in the first place, maybe you didn't think before you acted or maybe you were plain lazy and stupid. Whatever reason, it's OK! Learn from the experience and change whatever is needed. We can always choose to change paths... Make more realistic goals, create more focus, be more attentive, but most of all BE KIND TO YOURSELF!


HAPPY INT'L WOMEN'S DAY! OH MY!!! Where do I begin? You are all amazing beautiful women. Beauty comes from within! You can look beautiful on the outside, but if you don't do the work to find your beauty inside yourself, you are missing out in having a fulfilled life. We are all unique human beings! And that is why we should never be comparing ourselves to anyone else, other than us yesterday and how we want to be tomorrow! Women are naturally strong! I truly believe that God gave us the ability to bear a child in our wombs for a reason! PMS? Really? Going through that every month on its own, makes us heroes! For the women who have no kids today or that decided they don't want to ever have kids, I respect your choice, and everyone should too! But you ALSO have that strength that every woman who bears a child has. We are sensitive, we have intuition! We are BRAVE! Everyone has their own story of bravery. Don't let anyone diminish whatever your story is! It is YOUR story! I am also HONORED to have so many amazing women following me on this account and letting me know I inspire them! I want to inspire them to find within themselves the amazing woman that they ARE! I love you all and I hope you have an amazing day celebrating your WOMAN'S AMAZINGNESS!


PATIENCE IS A VIRTUE! I guess this is an old one, right? Well... let's spin it a bit: BEING PATIENT WITH OURSLEVES IS A TRUE VIRTUE! We have the tendency to be really hard on ourselves, more than we are with others. As women, multitaskers, mothers, friends, wives, employees, colleagues, we should give ourselves more credit for being able to be who we are, taking the time and patience to look inside and see the beauty we can bring to this world!


WHAT EXACTLY IS WEALTH? I spent about 5 super fun hours yesterday with my daughter walking in the Rodeo Drive area in Beverly Hills. You see a lot of "money" wealth and a lot of Botox and lip fillers. A lot of SUPERFICIAL WEALTH, as I would call it! The wealth I love is INNER WEALTH! It means being rich with your own emotions, the sharing of your gifts and being the best that you can be! What I call superficial wealth, doesn't bring real happiness to anyone! It can buy you "things", but it can't buy you happiness, health and love, which are the most important things in our lives. What is "wealth" for you?


HOW CAN YOU FIND YOUR PRINCE CHARMING? One has to be emotionally ready and available for the right prince to find you in your castle. And the best way to attract someone who will treat you like a princess, respect you like a gentleman and love you for who you are is to LOVE YOURSELF FIRST! I found my Prince Charming, actually he found me in a moment when I had finally figured out who I wanted to be after my divorce. I was ready and I loved myself! If you haven't found your prince charming yet, don't worry, keep loving yourself and he will show up when you least expect it!


DON'T CUT YOURSELF SHORT! Your life story could be as interesting and fascinating as the ones you see of people you follow on Instagram. I'm serious! It's all a matter of perspective. If you are diving in the fantasy of watching the lives of celebrities and people that are clearly showing the best of the best, you are creating a false reality to yourself. It's fun to watch and appreciate the dreamy vacations, amazing bodies, gorgeous outfits, perfect skin, make-up and hair, but this might get to a point that it can create a negative feeling about yourself, your life and YOU personally. I have no doubt you have amazing moments in your own life! REAL MOMENTS! Think about one of those moments right now as you read this message and hold it dear to your heart! Now you just need to find how to replicate it in different ways in your reality today! We have to live our own realities and be the happiest we can be, instead of desiring someone else's life, which is not our reality! That is certainly cutting your chances of being REALLY HAPPY!

People are always telling us: "LOVE YOURSELF". We hear this from every loved one and our Coaches, right? But the big question is "HOW DO I START?!" Start by treating yourself exactly how you treat your loved ones. Start telling yourself exactly the things you tell your loved ones when they need your words of encouragement. When you hear yourself giving that negative self-talk, STOP and think what you would tell your loved one if they had told you the same about themselves, i.e.: "mom, I hate my body!". What would you tell your daughter if she told you that? Why don't you tell yourself the same? Let's start NOW to treat yourself with the same love and care! Once we genuinely love ourselves for who we are, everything else in life flows better. We know our qualities and focus on those, but we need to understand our limitations, which we work to improve and accept what can't be changed or controlled! LOVE YOURSELF, BE YOU, BE AUTHENTICALLY YOU and life will be much better, I promise you that!

BE BRAVE! Create the habit of seeing what your reality is and not the perception of what others might think of you! I believe that being brave means being authentically you, following your morals and honoring your values. Believing in yourself and in the power of your mind. Creating a mindset that is true to who you are and following it no matter what with your daily actions. I love this message from Jay Shetty: "We live in a perception of a perception of ourselves. If I think you think I am smart, I feel smart. If I think you think I'm stupid, I feel stupid. We are basing our self-worth on a perception of a perception. That is someone else's subjective opinion that you don't even know. So, you are being subjective about someone's subjectivity! That way you forget your reality because you are lost in a perception within a perception within a perception". What does being BRAVE mean to you?

If you want to be SUCCESSFUL you have to BELIEVE IN YOURSELF, otherwise you have to count on everyone around you being unsuccessful for you to succeed. No one will do it for you! It's on you, ONLY YOU! You have to be persistent and understand that as long as you are seeing progress, growth is on its way! So, start believing that you can do it, stay on track, and you will succeed!

BE UNAPOLOGETICALLY YOU! When you are true to your values, true to yourself, authentic and real, your life can flow so much better! You will certainly feel more comfortable by just being who you are! Please don't ever change who you are for anybody! Learn how to love yourself, because I know you are amazing! All human beings are amazing! Find that amazingness in you and share it with the world! What would you love to share with the world today?!

How do you believe you earn respect from others? We all know that respect is earned, not imposed, right? I believe that to earn anyone's respect, you first have to respect yourself! Next, you certainly need to be respectful to others. But more important than anything is to be true to yourself, honest and real. How can you earn anyone's respect, if you don't respect yourself first? Respect your body, your mind, your reality, respect who you are! If you don't feel that way, you can make changes to your life that will get you there.

What about appreciating what you have instead of wishing for what you don't have? We have the tendency to think that the grass is greener in the neighbor's yard, don't we? Wishing for what you don't have won't change your life! Start appreciating what you do have and make changes and take action to achieve the things you want that will make you happier or more fulfilled! But comparing your life to other's and wishing for what you don't have is not changing your world. Appreciate and take action!

BEING DIFFERENT IS GOOD! What differentiates you from everyone else? Being different means that you are being your unique self! Authentic, not trying to "be like" anyone else! When you get to the point where you love yourself enough to share your gift with the world, bells will ring! Life will make more sense! Be proud to be your authentic self and never apologize for it!

"I DON'T HAVE TO RESIST THE TRUTH OF WHO I AM. I will start existing as my full and authentic self. My identity is not my obstacle. My identity is my superpower." America Ferreira. Understand your own truth and embrace it with all your heart! Improve what you believe will make you a better person. That will automatically bring out your authentic self! Who is the real you? If you lost her, go find her in your heart!

YOU CAN CHOOSE WHAT COLORS YOU WOULD LIKE YOUR LIFE TO BE! If you would like a colorful life, be colorful yourself.

How can you do that? By choosing to see and believe in the beauty of life itself, of human kind, believe in who YOU are! When we are happy in our own world, the colors pop up easily around us!

EXPECTING EXTERNAL VALIDATION WILL NOT BRING YOU WHAT YOU NEED. Looking inside, accepting who you are, embracing what you have and changing/improving what would make you a better version of yourself is what actually works, REALLY! Therefore, stop looking for external validation. You don't need it!

"IF YOU CAN LIFT UP YOUR VIEW OF YOURSELF, YOU CAN START TO CHANGE THE CULTURE THAT KEPT YOU DOWN." Melinda Gates. LOVE YOURSELF! Listen to your Leader Within, your positive voice. Not the negative voice that drags you down. It's just a matter of creating the awareness of the right voice! Inner work is what will lift you up!

"OUR CAPACITY TO LOVE AND CELEBRATE OTHER PEOPLE IS DIRECTLY CONNECTED TO OUR ABILITY TO FULLY LOVE OURSELVES!" Deepak Chopra. I love when I receive messages from other women complimenting me for anything they find that is beautiful or special in me! That makes me happy to receive the compliment, but most of all, it makes me super happy to see them "celebrating" another woman, because that means that they love themselves TOO! When a woman has a hard time celebrating other women, it's time for her to look inside to find and love that beautiful true self that I KNOW they have, because that is what will give them the ability to celebrate others.

ARE YOU HUMBLE ENOUGH to understand that we are the only ones that can develop, lift up and grow or fall, put down and spoil who we are as individuals? If you are feeling wronged and are blaming others for how they "broke" you, expecting that they will solve your hurt, and fix the wrong doing, think about it: maybe you are also wrong to think that way! No one will ever "break" you, unless you allow them to, and that is only because you will be breaking yourself up! The choice to accept that we are the sole responsibility for how we end up feeling, is the key to learning how to fix our own hurt! Don't ALLOW anyone to break you! Learn how to be strong by knowing who you are and loving yourself! People will bring tough feelings to your surface, but you can always choose to react to those feelings on your favor, which means: choosing not to allow yourself to be broken!

STOP LOOKING AROUND YOU. LOOK WITHIN TO FIND YOUR TRUE HAPPINESS AND JOY!
Who are you, REALLY? Nowadays with so much we see out there in social media, some people might lose their own sense of self. Stop wishing to be someone else, having that person's life or body or job or fashion style... use the inspiration these people might instill in you, to bring the best out of you! Find who you really are, and I assure you, you will find real joy in your life, because YOU ARE AMAZING JUST THE WAY YOU ARE!

DO YOU BELIEVE IN YOURSELF? ARE YOU WHERE YOU WANTED TO BE IN YOUR LIFE? Ask yourself this question: "What is stopping me from getting where I want to be in my life?" The biggest obstacle in our lives is surprisingly ourselves. We don't realize the power we have with our own minds, to believe in ourselves and move ahead with our wishes and dreams. And our hardships are actually a blessing (sounds weird to say doesn't it) because they will make the shift inside of us that will bring the biggest strength and inner power that we have. We always get surprised how strong we are after we "survive" a hardship in life, isn't it?

DON'T MEASURE YOUR WORTH BY HOW MANY HEARTS OR LIKES YOU GET or how many followers you have. If you feel the need for those likes & followers, consider that you are probably in pain somehow. Think that you are giving your power away to others!! You don't have to! You are asking others to tell you what your value is. When you are the authority in your own life, you don't have to give your power away. But how can you get that power? By learning how to love yourself, creating self-esteem, self-worth. Believing that you are enough! YOU ARE WORTHY! YOU DESERVE TO BE LOVED AND ACCEPTED THE WAY YOU ARE. But for that to happen, you have to love yourself first! Your True Self is powerful, creative and a loving spirit and that never changes!

**How is your self-love doing? What can you start doing today to improve that?**

_____

_____

_____

_____

_____

_____

_____

_____

_____

_____

_____

_____

_____

_____

_____

_____

_____

_____

# PARENTING & RELATIONSHIPS

*Being a parent is one of the most important jobs I've ever had in my life! The responsibility we have as parents to build the foundation for our kids' future as balanced adults is immense! There are so many different kinds of relationships: parents, kids, partners, friends, boyfriends/girlfriends, husband/wife, siblings... any of these relationships will work so much better if we practice self-love and self-awareness, as well as find ways to put ourselves in the other person's shoes. That is key! This is why I chose to add these motivational quotes after the previous 2 chapters. I hope the following quotes inspire you to think deeply about all of the relationships you have in your life*

I heard about this YouTuber, Lindy Tsang, and that she does amazing work helping people be the best version of themselves, so I bought her book to read about her story. She is an inspiration to many kids out there. You can be famous and, successful, but grounded, humble and helpful to others at the same time! After I finish reading, I will give it to my 13 years old to read... let's share the right message to our younger generation! Social media a lot of times sends the wrong message to them, so it's refreshing to read Lindy's story!

I LOVE being a mother! Being a mother of a teenager is not easy! It was not too long ago that they were still that naive, innocent little person. But what we have to remember is that all the morals and the values that we teach our kids, and we will continue to teach throughout their teenage years, will stick to their heads and follow them throughout their rough teenage journey! They are becoming their own person: independent, full of opinions and hopefully will turn into a happy, healthy, independent and strong adult! As moms what we can do is to be there to support them throughout their beautiful journey... and read a lot of books about helping them with that journey. We were not born knowing how to raise our kids!

Following the theme of Mother's Day Weekend, there is a saying in Brazil that goes like this: "Being a mother is suffering in paradise"! We work really hard to raise our little ones, so besides the amazing things that go with it, we also have a lot of tough situations we have to go through. So we cannot forget about ourselves in that journey... we have to be constantly doing something for ourselves! That will make us become a better/happier mom, and ready to take on what comes next, when our little ones, are no longer little and leave our nest!! Have you done something for yourself today that makes you feel fabulous?!

For some of us women, feeling fabulous after a divorce is really hard... we might feel like a failure, we feel lost and sometimes alone, even though we know there are people around us to support us... But the feeling is there, and it's hard to deal with. I understand people handle stress and crisis in different ways, but I wanted to share what worked for me. I focused on all the good things I had in my life and I worked hard to make sure my daughter did not suffer with me during this phase. This was my issue with her dad, not hers... Therefore, to this day, her dad and I do a great job in making sure we respect each other, and we work as parents of this beautiful girl, who we want to make sure grows to become a confident woman, who believes in love and respect!

Today is Father's Day in Brazil. I wish every human being understood how important the role of a father is, and of course the mother, in a child's life! The parents of a child are the ones who undoubtedly shape the adult that person is going to be...scary, isn't it? I have so much to thank my dad for the person that I am today. Honesty was always something he clearly taught us. But the love and attention I always had from both of my parents is what I believe gave me the confidence I have today to be proud of the woman that I became! They always believed in me! And they made sure I knew that all the time! A child needs to constantly feel loved and cared for by their parents. And when parents get divorced, both sides should make all the effort they can, to maintain and support the parent/child relationship their kids have with their ex-spouse. Once you have a child with another person, that is a life bond you will always have with them, even if you get divorced. You will have to work together for your kids' happiness and make sure to maintain the respect between each other. Your relationship with your ex-spouse and your current spouse, in case you remarry, will teach your kids how to relate to their own future spouse. That is A LOT of responsibility... think about it! Being a parent is being there for them forever, loving and caring. That doesn't mean saying yes to everything! To the contrary!! You will have to say a lot of NOs for your child to survive and learn right from wrong... Feliz dia dos Pais for all the fathers in Brazil!

Here is a quote that inspired me today: "The entire point of being alive is to evolve into the person you are meant to be." I would add to this quote by saying that besides evolving into who we were meant to be, we should also make sure that we engage with the right life partner, who will unveil our own perfect self, like a Michelangelo unfinished work of art, as if the sculpture emerges from the marble! Not someone who will try to change or reshape who you really are...

Sometimes we have new friends that show up in our adult lives and capture a big part of our heart! Last night I was celebrating one of these friends' birthday! We should always treasure the people who really care and treasure us! As an adult woman, the phase of teenage years when you are always struggling with your friendships is over. Time to make sure you spend quality time with quality people!

EXPECTATIONS... It's interesting how we create our own expectations of how we want others to react around us, but a lot of times: many, many times actually, we forget to share those expectations with that person, and we end up being disappointed, and upset with that person, when we did NOT need to be! At the end of the day, if we are not clear, it is actually our fault if we feel disappointed... The best thing to do is to create the habit of sharing with your personal and professional contacts what expectations you have from them, in a nice, respectful and clear manner. That will help both sides to understand what's at stake. In any case, that still doesn't mean you won't be disappointed. The other side might still not fulfill your expectations even after you made it clear to them. We are humans after all... And that is when a good old conversation to clarify the situation might be of help! As usual: COMMUNICATION IS THE KEY for a good relationship of any kind! "Trade your expectation for appreciation, and your life will change in an instant". Some food for thought! Maybe expect less, and appreciate more...

PERSPECTIVE... the way we feel about something, comes from our own perspective about life and all that happens with it! When I divorced, what hurt me the most at the time was thinking that my daughter was going to grow up with a "broken family". With an open heart and mind, I now see and realize that my daughter is lucky to have 2 loving families: my new husband and the family he brought to our world and my daughter's stepmom and the family she brought to Bella's world! As I said... it's all about perspective! HAPPY THANKSGIVING to you all! I am thankful every day, not only today for my big family, friends, health and all the opportunities the universe brings my way. I am also thankful for all the lessons I learned from what I didn't expect to happen in my life! I learn every day from everyone around me! Let's open our hearts and our minds to a more fulfilling life!!

FAILURE is one of the fastest ways of learning! Any action will lead to learning! Failing at any action, even failing to take action, is a rich learning opportunity. So "celebrate" your failures as special opportunities for learning! Meaning: we should have an appreciation for the experience... We end up learning more from what doesn't work than from what does work! I am not saying that we need to look for failure, but we should be open to the risk of failing, which is hard for a lot of people to accept. Let's be open to that kind of learning. As I always say, it's your own choice on how you react to what happens in your life!

Here is a tip if you are struggling to communicate with someone and you don't want to hurt each other... When I am angry or upset with someone, sometimes, instead of having a heated argument, I go to my paper and pen and start writing that person a letter. I take my time to take everything off my chest, which feels liberating to vent without hurting anyone or heating up someone else's ears. And taking the time to write, read and edit, the message will be clearer and then you can give the other person the chance to understand your thoughts without a heated conversation with interruptions. You also give that person a chance to do the same. I'd just be careful with what you put on paper, because once you send, you can't take it back and it's registered forever. Sometimes, you might just realize you don't need to send the letter after all, after your head clears and you read what you wrote a day after... But for certain situations, that might be exactly what you need!

Just got really emotional seeing these 2 tiny squirrels fighting in my back yard. One was being so mean, biting and attacking while the other was just trying to defend itself, but it was bitten really bad, when I was able to shoo the mean one away. But unfortunately, the little one didn't survive. It made me think that in our human world, there are people out there with the intent to harm us, but we should NOT be mean back. We are not animals and we 'hopefully' won't bite, so try to help them first... When someone is there to hurt you, remember they are most likely hurting a lot inside themselves... if you can't help the ones around you by being nice, just get away, because they will end up hurting you. There is always so much we can do, right? But the first thing we do should always be to try and help back. Let's try to be nice to each other...

"LEAD BY EXAMPLE" is a very important phrase for me! Actions certainly speak way louder than words! So if you want your kids, or your friends, your spouse or girlfriend/boyfriend, your partner to act a certain way around you, ask yourself if you are leading by example... it's always easy for us human beings to complain about others' attitudes toward us, but sometimes we don't notice that we might be acting the same way towards them... my point is that we should all be more conscientious about how we act around others and always try to lead by example, before asking someone to change their attitude towards us.

Truth is what you believe in! Your truth might be different than someone else's truth... I am not talking about facts, like "the grass is green". There is no argument about that! I am talking about beliefs and ideologies. Each person has their own beliefs and ideologies (their own truth), and they start building that at home with mom and dad, and that might change as they mature, and create their own life experiences. One should never impose their own truth onto others. What we can do is respectfully have a conversation and explain our own truth and maybe that might change the other person's opinion about that truth, but that's all we can do. Let's respect other people's truths and our own.

Saying "I'm sorry" might be really hard for some people. Maybe to acknowledge that you did something wrong, or the hardest part, for the fact that once you say: "I am sorry", you should be ready to put that behind you! I respect and admire people that genuinely say I am sorry and really follow through, by putting it behind them, because I know how hard that can be! But you know what? There is not a single person in this world that doesn't make mistakes and doesn't need to acknowledge, apologize, put it behind them and learn from the experience, isn't it true? If there is someone you keep thinking about saying "I'm sorry" to, because you know you have a reason to do so, go ahead and do it today! But when you do it, it only works if you really feel you can put that behind you! If you are not ready for that and still working on your feelings, don't do it until you are ready! But when you do it, you will feel a weight coming off your shoulders!

The most important thing in a relationship for me is RESPECT! Each individual has their own opinion about anything in life. The hard thing for most people is to respect and understand and sometimes accept that other person's opinion might be different than yours. When you meet someone or are talking to someone whose opinion is different than yours, listen, try to understand their point of view, and if you still don't agree, use your facts and arguments to demonstrate your own opinion, respectfully! You might even be able to convince them to agree with you. But if you don't, just respect they have a different opinion than yours and move on... sometimes, if the subject being discussed is a basic moral or value of yours, most likely, you both won't be able to relate in a healthy manner. But the respect should always be there!

The habit of texting someone about every single issue in your life can destroy your ability to react appropriately on an emotional crisis. I can see that with kids nowadays. They mostly communicate via text, so when they see themselves in a face to face situation, they can't type, fix, rewrite or ask a friend if what they want to say is OK. When you send someone a text about an emotional subject, certainly you will end up writing something you would never say face to face. There is also the fact that you can't see people's real emotions when reading what they sent you and you can't see their reaction to what you said or their reaction while saying something. Let's try to call or Facetime more instead of texting all the time. Try to use text for practical issues, not to express your emotions...
FORGIVENESS... Most people have at least one person in their lives that they feel they have to forgive, or they are told they need to forgive. The hurt that the person inflicted in you could

be used as the tool to find how to forgive... Don't think you will forget, because you won't... it will always be there in you, but your reaction to the hurt you feel, directly affects the ones around you who truly love you: your spouse, partner, kids, siblings, parents, etc... Maybe how the hurt in you might be affecting your loved ones. That can give you the strength to try and listen to the person who hurt you and understand what their truth is... maybe you will be able to find a way to forgive them and deal with your own hurt, so that you don't hurt your loved ones...

Are you really LISTENING? Our tendency is to jump to conclusions when someone is talking to us, by focusing on our own life experiences and our reaction to the words they are saying, isn't it?! What we forget is that true listening is removing all judgement from our own thinking and focusing on what the other person is actually trying to say, while not only listening to their words, but also paying attention to their body language and the inner message behind the words that are coming out of their mouth! Connect with their being, not the issue or the problem they are trying to convey. If you really listen, when you open your mouth to talk, you will be ready to have a much more open conversation! Do you think you actually listen when talking to others at home, at work, at school?

What are the LEARNING STEPS?
• Unconscious Incompetence: I don't know what I don't know
• Conscious Incompetence: Now I know what I don't know. When we first start learning a new skill or way of being in the world, it can be overwhelming to realize how much we don't know...
• Conscious Competence: I know what I know.
Having the ability to learn something in life is always a gift! The reality is that we learn from everything and everyone around us! Be smart and take it in all that life gives you and turn it into

a good lesson! Good or bad, there is always something we can learn from an experience and we can focus on the positives of that chance for learning something new!

There are different kinds of LOVE. The love I have for my siblings is very special to me! They are both my best friends, the ones I know will always be there for me and defend me from any harm! Sometimes to the point where we know we need to back off because we worry too much! That friendship, respect, interest, worry, etc. was all built throughout our childhood! We argue, we disagree, but we know we will always have the best intentions towards each other! I know this is not the same for everyone, but I wish and pray that everyone has this same feeling towards their siblings! What about giving you siblings some love today?

Should you FIND A SOLUTION or FIND A CULPRIT? When you have a problem to solve, spending all the time looking for whose fault it was will just delay the process of finding the solution of that problem! Instead of wasting time looking for who is guilty, spend time finding a solution! Of course, certain problems need to be viewed in a way that the person who created it helps to find the solution.

Will Smith once talked in a video about the DIFFERENCE BETWEEN FAULT & RESPONSIBILITY. It doesn't matter whose fault it is when something is broken. It's your responsibility to fix it. For example: it's not somebody's fault if they had some kind of abuse as a child, but it is their responsibility to figure out how they are going to deal with those traumas and try to make a decent life out of it. It's not your fault if your partner cheated on you and ruined your marriage as well as your plans for the perfect family, but it is for sure your responsibility to figure out how to take that pain and overcome it to build a happy life for yourself and your kids. It sucks that fault and responsibility do not go together, but they just don't! When something is somebody's fault, we want them to suffer, we want them punished, we want them to pay, we want it to be their responsibility to fix it, but that is not how it works, especially when it is your heart. Your life, your happiness. It is your responsibility, and your responsibility alone! When we are pointing the finger and stuck in whose fault something is, we are jammed and trapped into victim mode. When you are in victim mode, you are stuck in suffering. The road to power is in taking responsibility. Your heart, your life, your happiness is your responsibility and your responsibility alone! Take back your power by taking responsibility to fix your own heart!


On Valentine's Day I want to talk about REAL LOVE! When you REALLY LOVE someone, your feelings towards that person end up being selfless! You love them for who they are, how they are, for how they make you feel, for what they mean to be part of your world! That being said, you will always want to see that person happy, right? You will do anything you can to bring that smile to their face, and you don't ask anything in return, because you just REALLY LOVE them! That's how I feel about my husband! Todd, you mean the world to me, and I love you selflessly and can't wait every day to see that beautiful smile on your face! TE AMO MEU AMOR! Happy Valentine's Day!


Being a mother is one of the hardest jobs I've ever had and at the same time, the most rewarding by far! My mother gave me the amazing foundation I needed to become the mother that I am today! She gave me the attention, discipline, support and unconditional love, that certainly molded me to be a good mom to Bella. Mãezinha, Feliz dia das Mães! Você é maravilhosa! Te amo!

Happy Mother's Day to all of you amazing moms out there who a lot of times don't realize how good of a mom you are!

CONFLICT IS THE ESSENTIAL INGREDIENT IN ALL SUFFERING. INNER AND OUTSIDE CONFLICT. When you are having inner conflict, you should ask yourself what exactly you are observing, what are you feeling, what do you really need and finally what is the best way to fulfill this need. Be honest and true to yourself. For outside conflict, remember that there is the perception of injustice in BOTH sides... learn to forgive yourself and the other, not because the other person needs forgiveness, but because you need emotional peace!

It's Father's Day in the U.S. today, but not in Brazil. Happy Father's Day to Bella's dad and Bella's step dad! I decided to write this post to share a message with all the mothers out there who are divorcing or have been divorced, to hopefully inspire them to understand that the relationship between their kids and their father is essential for their kids' mental and emotional health. As much as their relationship with you, the mother! It's important to think about that when deciding on any attitudes you are taking or whatever things you think of doing that might affect that relationship. Always make sure to treasure, empower and support the relationship between your kids and their father. And it's very important to try and separate that from whatever is going on between mom and dad. It shouldn't matter if there is animosity, if it is someone's fault or not... the issues between mom and dad should stay between mom and dad. Therefore maintaining, supporting and empowering the love and the relationship between the kids and their father is key for these kids to become healthy adults!

"YOU HAVE A "FABULOUS" SPIRIT OF LOVE AND MATURITY SO MANY FAMILY'S HURT BY DIVORCE DO NOT HAVE. LOVE MOM".

I just received this text message from my ex-mother-in-law, whom I still call mom., so this message made me teary eyed and I would like to share with you ladies who are getting divorced or have already gotten divorced, a message I hope can be enlightening to your life path: "when you get divorced, you are dealing with and affecting a lot of people from the 2 families involved who will forever be connected if you have kids. That will never change. When you do your best to see a situation through the other person's perspective, through their own eyes, you will end up having more empathy and be able to bring your loving self and your natural maturity to the front. Being humble and understanding that the world doesn't revolve around only you, even though this might be the most painful moment in your life, is what will give you the maturity to find a way to put yourself on the other person's shoes. I promise you that when you have empathy and think of others as well as yourself, even in your darkest moments, your life path will definitely be smoother and everyone around you will feel the same.


DO YOU WANT QUALITY IN YOUR LIFE? CREATE QUALITY RELATIONSHIPS! Here are 9 great strategies on how to build healthy relationships by Deepak Chopra:
1. Listen and Be Present
2. Practice Non-Judgement
3. Create Healthy Boundaries
4. Give and Receive
5. Schedule Quality Time Together
6. Schedule Quality Time Apart
7. Communicate Consciously (when you are emotionally charged, ask yourself the following questions and then share the answers with your partner: 1-what happened? 2-What emotions am I feeling? 3-what do I need that I am not receiving? 4- what am I asking for?)

8. Actively Love (practice doing things to demonstrate your love)
9. Be Authentic (that also means being vulnerable)


Today is National Daughter's Day! What can I say about my adorable Bella?! I went through 2 miscarriages before Bella came to this world. She was born a preemie at 32 weeks. She was an angel baby! She brings me so much joy that I sometimes have to pinch myself to believe she is mine! I am so proud of the young woman she is turning out to be: responsible, super talented, loving, funny, tall, very tall! Bella Wierson, I love you more than any words can say, and I am very grateful for having YOU as my daughter, my only daughter! And my wish for you is that you become a woman who is confident, happy and capable of creating a life for yourself that will bring you joy every single day to you and everyone around you! You are my GEM.


NO ONE IS PERFECT!
How many times have you heard this phrase? But people still expect that their partner in life be a "perfect" partner. If you want a perfect partner, jump into a fairy tale book and become a character. If you want joy in your real life, BE REAL! There is no such thing as perfection. There are human beings working towards their own goals to find joy and happiness in their lives. What you have to do is be aware of who your partner is, make an effort to really understand them and appreciate every single thing they have as a quality that adds to your relationship. The things you don't appreciate, COMMUNICATE, but do it with respect and the right intention of understanding where they are coming from. I feel blessed to have found a partner that I love, and I appreciate all the qualities he has which made me fall in love with him in the first place! Remember that, cherish that and REPEAT the good moment in different versions!

**Make a list of the things you want to change today to become a better parent as well as improve all the relationships you have in your life!**

_____

_____

_____

_____

_____

_____

_____

_____

_____

_____

_____

_____

_____

_____

_____

_____

_____

_____

_____

# HEALTHY HABITS

*To create a healthy life for ourselves, we need to create healthy habits, and get rid of the unhealthy ones. How can we do that? By being aware when we are acting on a bad habit and starting a new habit right away. We always have a choice to do things differently. Sometimes we just need to change our perspective by looking at our life and at certain situations with different eyes.*

Why wait if you don't have to?! When you have a plan to accomplish something in your life and all the stars are aligned, but you see yourself still not moving forward, it's time to ask yourself what is holding you back! Sometimes we are our worst critic, and we end up making it hard for ourselves to be successful! Other times, we worry too much about what others say about us, right?! If you have that project you really want to accomplish, but can't make it move forward, make it a point TODAY to write down a list of the reasons why it's not moving ahead... and that will make you rethink all the details and you might actually realize you need more time and work, or you might determine that you are ready to move on!! One thing is for sure: when something is stuck in our lives, any tiny step makes a difference!! Take charge of your own future today!!!

Being productive is not a gift it's a habit you create! You can choose to be productive. You can start by creating the habit of starting an early morning routine, to set the tone for the rest of your day!! It could be as simple as making your own bed right after you wake up, reading the news, doing some exercise, meditating, or anything that gives you energy and some sense of accomplishment! Most likely you will not have the will or the time to do that routine every single day. We all know that no one's life is perfect! But you can build your own life with the intention to do your best every day! The truth is that there is no magic! What really exists is hard work, being realistic and taking advantage of what is actually real in your life! You should never feel sorry for yourself. Playing the victim doesn't help anyone. You can choose to be productive! Build that habit for yourself!

Being fit and looking healthy is all a matter of choice! I choose to be fit and healthy! There is no magic or secret! You just have to choose a healthy lifestyle and have discipline! Remember that it is all about balance! If you are still on your journey to reach your goal, you will for sure have to work a bit harder, than someone who is already there! Maintaining a fit body is not so hard after you reach your goal! I can still eat my dessert sometimes, or drink my wine, as long as I continue my discipline of eating and drinking mostly healthy food: colors and flavors! And I keep exercising as many times a week as I can. If I can't work out for a few days, I know I'll be OK if I don't overindulge on food and drinks! As I said, it's all about the choices you make! Do you want to choose to be healthy and fit?!! Go for it!!

We are the ones who create our BAD HABITS. Therefore, we are also the only ones who can create the awareness of those bad habits. THAT is the key to breaking them! When you find yourself in that special moment of awareness, celebrate and break the bad habit once and for all. The strength that we have in our own minds to control our destiny is so powerful and a lot of us don't realize that. So, let's make an effort to become more aware?! Remember we have a choice in everything we do! YES WE DO!!

FITNESS GOALS! This is not your typical transformation picture! Let's be real here! Being fit is not simple or easy! It includes hard work, dedication, focus and consistency! It's a lifestyle, really!!! It's a choice, like anything else in your life!! If you really choose to be fit and make it a priority, it will happen! There are levels of fitness, so choose the one that you can stick with and stay consistent, so you don't end up giving up! Left picture was about 5 years ago, when I was very strict with my diet and I was 8lbs leaner and more fit, but I was not happy without my wine and ice cream! The other one was a couple of weeks ago, with a balanced/happy life where I look less lean, but I feel good that I can eat and drink what I want, in moderation of course, but I am still consistent with my workouts.

EXCUSES are something that we all create... the reality is that when we want something, or really have the need or the desire to do something, we will find a way! Hopefully the right way. One of the human needs that will actually create fulfillment to a human being, as per Tony Robbins, is the need for growth! It is growth that creates progress in our life. If you have the goal to be more fit in the new year, actually whenever you really want it, try being aware when you start creating excuses! I found 20 minutes of my vacation yesterday by the pool to do my workout, because I want to stay fit! What about you?! Anything holding you back?

NEW YEAR's RESOLUTIONS... instead of making people excited to make good changes in their lives for the new year, it stresses people out. Most of the time, it's just a list that never leaves your desk, drawer or kitchen counter, right? If you really have a few things, or even a lot of things you want to improve in your life, choose ONE! Only one thing, you know you can stick to and work on making progress towards your goal without pressure! BE REALISTIC! If losing weight is one of your resolutions, start little by little, making smart trades, like drinking sparkling water like La Croix, instead of soda, or substitute honey or agave for sugar... these small changes will already make a small difference. That way it's easier to keep it up! Take your time with whatever goals you have for the year. You have 365 days to make all the changes you want! What is your ONE goal for 2019?!

BALANCE is everything, right? I say this a lot, because it is so true!! Yesterday I enjoyed eating and drinking whatever I wanted, things that would not be part of my normally healthy diet! But I am on vacation and I was feeling like having that coconut sugary candy, a Chinese noodle box and a couple of glasses of wine while playing a board games with my family! Today I am enjoying the beach and added a beach workout and a 20 min run on the sand to feel good about myself. If you are too restrictive with your diet at all times, the chances are higher you will not be able to keep it up... therefore, if you have to let go for a day, do it and enjoy, do NOT feel guilty the next day. Just go back to your routine and make smart choices.

Create that balance that will allow you to have a lifestyle you can sustain!


Many TIME MANAGEMENT STRATEGIES often focus on time itself. How long is it taking you to complete something? Are you getting enough done in the amount of time you have? This strategy requires you to focus on the activity, or the action that you're trying to complete, rather than the result, or the outcome you desire. By focusing on the task at hand, you distract yourself from what really matters, which is the outcome or what you're getting for your time. When you forego time effective time management strategies and get bogged down in to-do lists, it leads you down a path of frustration and the feeling that you're overwhelmed. The best strategies for time management involve finding a way of thinking that focuses on what matters most to you, which is your purpose!


The importance of CONSISTENCY! Everything you do that requires action, will also require consistency for a successful outcome! Like brushing your teeth every day, is the only way to keep your teeth healthy, right? Even to build a healthy relationship and have your new partner fall in love with you, you have to be yourself, and act consistently in the way that person will fall in love with you little by little for who you actually are! We don't fall in love overnight! Reaching your fitness goals is no different! Going to the gym once a month for 5 hours and eating bad food instead of a consistent clean diet will NOT give you results. It's not about single intense events, but about consistency! The results happen with the consistency of your daily actions! And it's OK to screw up sometimes if you go back to being consistent after that! Don't be hard on yourself! Take action and be consistent!

REAL TRANSFORMATION HAPPENS FROM WITHIN! Even if your objective is only to change your body, adjusting to a new diet, creating discipline and keeping focused to reach your goal, will only happen if you first have a transformation of your mindset and daily habits, right? Most transformations happen when we are so sick of whatever is going on in our lives that we finally decide to take action! The picture above is deceiving, isn't it? I am not showing much of a physical change... They are about 4 years apart. The biggest transformation happened from within! On the left, I was in one of the most vulnerable moments in my life, a few months from my divorce. The one on the right, I had recently remarried my current amazing husband! The transformation that I see from these 2 pictures is a stronger woman that learned many lessons that I will hold for life, and that is what I consider real transformation.

WHEN WAS THE LAST TIME YOU LAUGHED at yourself or at something you thought was really funny?! I love when I bring out the goofy in me and enjoy laughing at myself! I love laughing, period! Laughter decreases stress hormones and increases immune cells and infection-fighting antibodies, thus improving your resistance to disease. Laughter triggers the release of endorphins, the body's natural feel-good chemicals. Endorphins promote an overall sense of well-being and can even temporarily relieve pain. So guys, what are you waiting for! Laugh more!! Laugh often. Not LOL emoji laughs, REAL LAUGHS!

THE ENVIRONMENT WE LIVE IN is everything! For you to grow in any way, you need to be living in an environment that is conducive for that growth to happen! The way to create a safe environment for ourselves is to create clear boundaries personally and professionally around us, and to focus on our morals and values. As Eleanor Roosevelt said: "No one can make you feel inferior without your consent"! I would add to that the fact that you can choose who you have in your life, who will create the environment you live in! Time to clean up that contact list and keep in it only people who you believe can add/share value in your life in one way or another! We work hard to create boundaries for our kids. We can't forget to build our own!

What does BEING POSITIVE mean? I consider myself a very positive person. That doesn't mean I don't feel sad, upset or sometimes have negative thoughts. I do! But my nature tells me to brush them off with positive reaction to the negative feelings and thoughts. It's our choice, really! For example, instead of saying to yourself: "I'm not going to make it", say "I tried my best and it will work, if it doesn't, I'll figure out something else, but will keep my positive thoughts and good energy flowing". Well... if you DIDN'T do your best, then you could say that you won't make it, not because you are being negative, but because you are being realistic, right? So, try this today: every time you have a negative thought, try finding a positive one, reframe it!

FOCUS ON WHAT YOU WANT AND NOT ON WHAT YOU DON'T WANT! When you are trying to solve a problem, what exactly are you focusing on? Are you focusing on the problem itself, on what you DON'T want or are you focusing on what you DO want? Think about that... What do you REALLY WANT? Are you seeing the opportunities or only the obstacles in front of you? Are you focusing on the problem or on the solution? We should focus on what needs to happen, on where we actually want to go, how to get back into the right direction, right? The tendency is to focus on the problem, on what scares us, instead of focusing on where we want to go and what you need to do. This is how you will certainly find the solution!

IT'S NOT ABOUT THE GROWTH, IT'S ABOUT THE PROGRESS! Growing continuously and contributing continuously is where the joy is! Progress = Happiness. If you don't meet your goal, but you see that you have made progress, you will be excited. But when you achieve the goal, you will feel good for a short period of time, because the purpose of the goal is not to get it. It is so that we become something more! If we achieve a goal that does not make us more, we will be really unfulfilled. That's why when you achieve a goal, you go to the next, because it's not about the goal. It's about the progress, and that is what creates the growth.

"A real decision is measured by the fact that you've taken a new action. If there is no action, you haven't truly decided" Tony Robbins. How true is this? You realize you are wrapping yourself up in your own indecisiveness when you "say" you want to do something, but it ends up never getting done. Sounds familiar? For anything to happen in our lives, we need to take action! Do something to create that progress that will take us to the point where we reach our goal! But not taking action, could be directly connected to us not having decided if we really want to achieve that specific goal... food for thought!

"EVERYONE HAS A HAPPY ENDING. IF YOU ARE NOT HAPPY, IT'S NOT THE END." Hmmm... that one made me think a little... this could easily NOT be true, right? But we could add a phrase at the end to make it better: "IF YOU CHOOSE SO!" Remember you always have a choice to create your own story, build your own future! If you believe you are not happy today, think about what would make you happy, and work towards it. It takes ACTION for anything to change and for different emotions to flow! Happiness is not going to happen when you have specific "things" in your life. Happiness is a state of mind. CHOOSE TO BE HAPPY and you will feel happy!

Each individual has their own relationship with exercise and eating habits, right? I exercise because I want to feel healthy, energized and it is the way I "meditate" by taking the time for myself and focusing only on the exercise itself, and nothing else. As a bonus, I feel pretty. The reality is that I do feel much better when I work out at least 3 times a week. It's always our choice to follow a healthy diet and exercise regime or not. Being healthy is always my choice. I want to live many years to see my daughter get married and have kids. I want to enjoy many trips around the world with my husband, and for all that I need to be healthy. The physical aspect of it as I said before is certainly a bonus.

TIMING IS EVERYTHING! It's not just about what you are doing, it's really about WHEN you are doing it that can make all the difference – letting you become the best version of yourself at work and at home. I listened to a podcast with Daniel Pink, a NYT best-selling author who talks about the 3 stages during the day that 80% of humans go through every day, and what helps us decide the TIMING of our daily tasks to be more efficient: PEAK during early morning, when we are most vigilant, is when we should do work that requires focus and attention! TROUGH during the early to mid-afternoon, is a very bad time when our brain power is very low... that's when we should do work like Admin stuff, that doesn't require brain power! And RECOVERY during late afternoon, early evening, is when our mood is good, but we are not vigilant, so that is a good time for brainstorming, creative activities! Let's be smarter in choosing WHEN we will do our daily tasks!

Sometimes when we are facing a challenge we don't even know where to start. Here are some tips to help you in OVERCOMING CHALLENGES. 1. BE FLEXIBLE instead of taking the approach of ALL OR NOTHING!
2. TAME YOUR INNER CRITIC, your negative voice. Become aware when your negative voice is the one talking to you and focus on what you REALLY want to do or to happen. Listen to your positive voice. It is always there waiting for you to listen to it!
3. REBOOT. Toss out the goals that are not working and start with fresh ones
4. LEARN FROM YOUR MISTAKES: "fail forward".
5. Embrace your PROBLEMS AS OPPORTUNITIES TO LEARN something, rather than dwelling on the "mistake".
Now good luck in overcoming your challenge. I know you can do it!

Doesn't it feel amazing when you help someone feel good about themselves? When something is going bad in their lives and they feel that they are in a very dark moment, you come and help them see things clearly. You can help them to continue feeling good about themselves despite the hardship they are going through! Sometimes when we are in a dark moment, it's hard to see things clearly! We might even hate ourselves at that point. Someone from outside the situation, who really cares for you, can help you see things clearly, like a rainbow that shows up behind the clouds after a big storm! That happens in our lives too! After dark moments, a rainbow will show up, if you are open to see it! Why not try to be the rainbow in someone else's life today?


Feeling young is a matter of choice! I am turning 48 next week and I feel young! Here are the things I believe make the biggest difference in what makes me feel young at almost 50:
1. I take care of my body by exercising regularly and eating healthy, giving it the right fuel it needs to grow older gracefully...
2. I make a point to be around people that care about me, that bring good energy to my life. People that bring the best out of me. They appreciate being around me.
3. I learned how to love myself with no apologies. I work to become a better person every day, and I know for a fact that perfection is not reality. Being perfect is what you want it to be...
4. Keep making new friends! Real friendships fill our lives with joy!
5. For us ladies, if you want to look physically young, you will have to do the work of taking care of your skin, your hair, etc. Do what makes you feel good about yourself. Don't do anything just to please others. It's about YOU!
6. Make your environment a healthy one.
What do you do to make you feel young? Maybe I can learn a few other ways


Research shows that people who fully feel joy have one thing in common: GRATITUDE! So, if you practice being grateful every day, you will certainly feel more joy in your life! I was always grateful for the big and obvious things in my life like health, love and family. But I'm talking about trying to be grateful for the littlest things that you normally would take for granted, like enjoying a warm cup of coffee or your warm bed, or even the warm sun on your skin after a long winter! That way, the joy comes naturally, I promise! Here's a challenge: write below 3 things you were grateful for today that otherwise you would take for granted? Remember, the little things!

"Your mind controls your brain, your brain controls your body, so if you want a healthy body, you need a healthy mind. You are, and you become what you think". I read this one on my trainer's Instagram today. So, let's think positive thoughts! Let's focus on the good! Let's not worry about what we CAN'T control and start managing what we CAN control. Your thoughts are totally under your control! You can control your reactions to your difficult emotions. They will still hurt, but you can focus on how you can handle them with positive energy. KEEP YOUR MIND UNDER CONTROL! You can do it!

Are you the type of person that talks a lot and at times with a lot of clarity about your dreams but actually never follows through? Does it resonate? Or are you a hungry person who will act on everything you believe will get you closer to your dreams? That is the big difference between the ones who succeed from the ones who don't! Take ACTION, create discipline and have attitude! Go ACT on your dreams and stop JUST dreaming!

What is your explanation for not following a healthy lifestyle? Most of us adults have a busy schedule, principally when we work and have kids and a house to manage. But one thing is certain: we MUST create some time for ourselves every day, to keep our mental and physical health! I choose to workout at home. Choose an exercise routine that works for you. Taking care of yourself and making healthy food choices will automatically create a healthy lifestyle for you! Choose to be healthy!

I believe that a good way to reduce division in the world is to learn how to respectfully disagree with people who think differently than you and doing hands on work if you want to make changes to existing laws/rules. Complaining and disrespecting others will NOT create change. Each individual has their own truth, the way they see the world and how they come up with their opinions. Be curious and respectful and act on what you believe you have the power to change! Who have you learned from this year and what changes have you made which you believe could improve your world?

What does "feeling healthy" and "looking good" mean to you? Our perception of what feeling healthy and looking good means is our own! Perfection in my opinion is very individual. Meaning that what we believe to be "perfect" might be totally different than others. Which is fine, because it's our life! Just remember to create realistic expectations about yourself AND others. We all think differently, and that is the beauty of human kind! We can ALWAYS learn from others! Including people you least expect to learn lessons from... What person surprised you with a lesson you never imagined you would learn from them?

YOUR THOUGHTS CAN HEAL YOUR BODY, YOUR MIND AND YOUR SOUL! The power of our thoughts is super strong! You can be and create whatever you want if you put your mind to it! Remember to be realistic, while appreciating and exploring the world around you. But when you focus on the positive and right thoughts, you can even heal your body. There are a lot of studies about that. And when you have your mind focusing on exactly what you are looking to accomplish, with action and the right attitude, the chances of you achieving them are really high!

"FORGIVENESS IS NOT AN ACTION OR THOUGHT. IT'S A SPIRITUAL QUALITY OF HEALING, THAT IS SUPPORTED BY THE LIGHT OF HOPE GROWING WITHIN US." Deepak Chopra. Giving and receiving forgiveness is an essential step in finding emotional freedom. I know it's not easy, but if you use your hope, together with compassion in your heart, it is possible! Hope is powerful to help control your feelings of resentment and despair. Stop listening to the voice of blame, resentment and punishment. These feelings are false perceptions of our ego self. Feed your hope!! It gives us courage!

DON'T FEEL BAD IF YOU MISS A WORKOUT OR TWO OR THREE. If you have been consistent but can't workout for a few days because of a busy schedule, there is no need to feel guilty. Get back on track as soon as you can and try keeping the healthy diet in place. Working out should be fun and not feel like it's a bad job you are obligated to do!

FAKE IT UNTIL YOU MAKE IT... DO YOU BELIEVE THAT WORKS?! We all have heard this phrase many times, right? I guess it does have a couple of outcomes here:
1. You know you are capable, but circumstances won't let you show/prove it yet, so you know you WILL make it and it's just a matter of time
2. You have a lot of self-doubt and are not sure you will actually make it, but you will fake it to try and be successful anyway, but in this example, you will certainly fall flat on your face and NOT be successful at all. I guess that if you are authentic, and have a

real plan, the word fake can be removed from the phrase to become: "WORK IT UNTIL YOU MAKE IT"


WHAT ARE THE SUMMER VIBES? Bikini season gets everyone focused on "getting ready" for the Summer. People start diets, workouts and doing what they can to fit well in that bikini fading in the back drawer by the time Summer is here. Don't you agree that most women want to look good in a bikini? I would change that phrase to "feel good in your own skin" in a bikini! Being focused and inspired to reach a realistic goal is key! You know what you can do and what makes you feel good about yourself! Stop comparing yourself with other women with "perfect" bikini bodies. Each woman is beautiful the way they are. Even more if they are clearly comfortable in their own skin! If you don't feel comfortable in your own skin today, work hard to reach your realistic goal. There is no magic to having a healthy body! It just means making the right food choices and exercising!


Having toned Abs happens 90% in the kitchen! You can do 1,000 crunches a day, but if you don't eat clean, the nice muscles will be hidden behind your fat. I used to have a real 6 pack, showing all muscles, but that only happened when I did not drink alcohol, or the mint chocolate chip ice cream like I had last night. It's a commitment that I am not into at this point. I am happy with my flat tummy without the six pack!


"The reason why women have to lift each other up, is not to replace men at the top of the hierarchy, but to become partners with men in ending hierarchy" Melinda Gates. Let's be the agents of change and convince the men to join in! Instead of being worried about women competing against you, lift them up and work hard, with honesty and using your real skills to win if there is a valid reason to "compete". There is no such thing as being "equals" we are ALL unique!

INDEPENDENT - first of 23 definitions: Not influenced or controlled by others in matters of opinion, conduct, etc.; thinking or acting for oneself. How independent are you?! I actually believe it's healthy to listen to others, but only agree with their opinion for the right reasons.

PERFECT EXCUSES CREATE PERFECT FAILURES! Sunday is supposed to be a rest day! But I felt like moving my body to bring in some energy from endorphins. The reality is that there is always an excuse we can find NOT to exercise, right? But the result of not moving your body, is not the same as if you do! As simple as that! If you move your body every day, doing what YOU enjoy doing, and eating healthy, is all you need for real healthy results. It's your choice! What are you going to choose?

"WHEN WE ALLOW OURSELVES TO BE FREE, THE OUTCOME MUST BE JUST THAT!" It IS that simple! When was the last time you felt free? Free from any outside pressures that go against your own values! Go back and remember how you were feeling and how good it is to just BE YOURSELF and not expect or worry about outside validation! BE TRUE TO YOURSELF, BE FREE, BE HAPPY!

IT'S MONDAY! THE DAY A LOT OF PEOPLE WANT TO START MAKING CHANGES IN THEIR LIVES... Are you one of those? That is great, but it only works if there is Action, AND if the action is CONSISTENT! For any changes to happen, like starting an exercise routine or a diet, you need to create a consistency by progressing little by little. TINY STEPS is the key. Start making the small changes you know you can keep consistent, then once it turns into a habit, move on to the next step. PROGRESS = HAPPINESS, I've said that before

HOW CAN YOU REALLY FORGIVE SOMEONE? Remember that when 2 people are going through a conflict, both sides are feeling injustice. The key to forgiveness is to create empathy for the other person and be humble enough to see that when you are trying to blame them, that is your own ego talking. Try to see things from a compassionate heart and use your power of hope for a better future, to bypass the revenge "fantasies". When you forgive someone, you are doing more for yourself than to them! You are creating peace for your own heart!

TRY TO HAVE FUN WHILE WORKING OUT! I believe that to create a healthy lifestyle, we need to not only eat healthy, but also to exercise as many times a week as we can. Creating the habit is key! For some people, who are not very fond of exercising, it's really hard to create that habit and be consistent. Why not try to find an exercise where you can have fun while doing it? I actually love working out, but on days I am not in the mood (yes, we all have those days) I put on music that really makes me want to dance!! And I actually dance in between exercises and I end up adding some cardio without even noticing.

THE ONLY THING YOU CAN CONTROL IN LIFE IS HOW YOU RESPOND TO LIFE. You have to let go of all those feelings that are festering in your heart so that you can move on! Free your mind to free your life...but how Fabiana?! The solution to resentment/bitterness is acceptance. Accept that what happened cannot be changed. What you can change is how you react to the situation from now on... also, the remedy to anger is love and empathy! Try to put yourself in the other person's shoes. Listen to them with no judgement! The reality is that we

93

act with anger and resentment when there is FEAR going on in our heart... maybe it's time for you to ask yourself: What am I afraid of? What are the real facts here, so that I am no longer fearful? Find your path to emotional freedom!

WHEN WE DON'T FORGIVE SOMEONE, the resentment, anger and "unforgiveness" is living within us. Negative emotions and subconscious beliefs, besides real trauma, can lead up to a real disease. These feelings create stress factors that generate chemical imbalance in our bodies... the pain you are inflicting in your body can go away as long as you take charge of how you react to your emotions. Once more I will say to you: focus on what you CAN control, not on what you CAN'T... Forgiveness is the greatest access to letting go! It's not about the other person. About letting them off the hook for what they've done or how they hurt you. It's helping YOU heal. When you start to let go of that inner judgement of the other person, and your victim mindset, you will recognize that life is actually working FOR you and not against you, you will generate healing! Do you have anyone in your world you need to forgive today? Think about it. It will be good for you, your mind and your overall health!

FEAR is what gets you stuck, preventing you from moving on in most things in life. Instead of being afraid of failing, turn this around and be afraid of the opposite: "what happens if you don't take action?" When you see the stakes are higher if you DON'T move on, then you have no reason for the fear, and it will be easier to move on. If the answer tells you that moving on can affect negatively many things in your life, then maybe there is a valid reason for the fear, and that will give you a chance to reevaluate your choices in the situation. You always have choices!

I have dual citizenship now! Brazilian and American! It's

incredible how a culture can mold someone's attitudes towards many things in life. Having lived in Brazil for 29 years and here for almost 20 now, I can say by experience that YES, a culture can mold your attitudes because of your old conditioning, but it's your choice, as an adult, to verify with your own eyes and experience, what part of that "culture" you actually want to keep, the part that doesn't go against your values, against what you truly believe! One clear and simple example is that Brazilians are well known for always being late, VERY late. But I never liked or followed that culture. One of my top values is RESPECT, and for me, when I am late, I am not respecting whomever I agreed to meet. Therefore, I chose to do it my way! My message is: follow your heart, honor your values, don't just believe in what your old conditioning is telling you. You can choose to do what you believe is right for you! Even if it is not what everyone else does.


URGENT vs IMPORTANT. IMPORTANT is something that has significance, that has value for you. Something that probably has a big effect on your success, survival or well-being. URGENT is something that requires immediate attention or action. Whether this is important or not depends on the significance it has in your life. Therefore, many urgent things for some will not necessarily be urgent to others because of the personal value they actually attribute to it.
What is your opinion about what you see as being the difference between URGENT and IMPORTANT?!


LEARN HOW TO SAY "NO"! Are you one of those people that cannot say NO? Acting that way will end up overwhelming you in a negative way. Here is a great tip to help you: when someone asks you something that you know the answer should be NO, just say "NO, I CAN'T", or "NO, I WON'T", or whatever is an appropriate answer to the question. But say that with a nice facial expression, and tone of voice that you feel bad but have no other choice. Then STOP THERE! If you start trying to explain yourself why you are saying no, you are giving the person the chance to try to convince you to say yes, since they most likely already know that you can't say NO. You can give them an alternative solution if you feel that's appropriate, like "I can't tomorrow, but I can check on my calendar and see a day that works for me and I'll let you know". Remember what your priorities are... their wish or your wish? It's your life, take control of it!

OUR BELIEFS CREATE OUR OWN REALITY. BELIEVE IN YOURSELF AND CREATE THE REALITY THAT YOU REALLY WANT IN LIFE! A belief is a thought we hold to be true. We create our own beliefs through the interpretation of our past experiences. We create the world that comes from our beliefs. Which means you can change whenever you CHOOSE to! If your old beliefs no longer serve your current reality create new ones! Believe in who you are TODAY! Believe that you CAN do whatever you put your mind to, always being realistic and understanding that you can change a belief in tune with your existing reality! We grow older, we evolve, we learn from our own mistakes and from others' and we CAN create and CHOOSE new beliefs, ultimately truly believing in ourselves.

FEAR vs CONSCIOUSNESS. Don't act out of fear. Act out of consciousness. Think if your fear is realistic. What are the facts? What are the chances that what you fear might actually happen? And if it does? How will it actually affect your life and in what ways? Consciousness is an interpretation. Our mind is interpreting the environment around us. So, we have the choice to change our perception, our mindset, change our belief about life, change our environment. And that way, we'll be sending that message to our body via our neuro systems. It's real... "WHAT WE THINK IS WHAT WE BECOME". Therefore, I'm telling you that you DO have the ability to change your environment and you have the ability to change your perception of the environment, which in the end can change your overall health. Our subconscious is another story... that is where fear comes from!! It comes from downloading other peoples' behaviors in our first 7 years of life. Mother, father, siblings, your community, our culture, our environment etc. You can also change that by the lessons you've learned in life as an adult. Choose to act out of consciousness, not fear!

"DON'T CHASE PEOPLE, be yourself, do your own thing, and work hard. The right people – the ones who really belong in your life – will come to you and stay..." Will Smith. Are you trying hard to chase that guy you believe is the right one for you? Or that friend you really want to hang out with? Think about it... if you are "chasing" someone, that means the relationship is one sided to start with. When you are authentically you, minding your own interests and joy in life, the right people will show up and meet you where you are! There is no magic in finding the right partner or the right friend. When you are real to your own way of being, your own morals and values, not "trying' hard to impress anyone, the right people WILL find you. I've seen that happening many times in my life. Just be REAL, be YOU and LOVE and FRIENDSHIP will come your way.

**What are the habits you know you need to change and what are the healthy habits you want to create?**

_____

_____

_____

_____

_____

_____

_____

_____

_____

_____

_____

_____

_____

_____

_____

_____

_____

_____

_____

_____

# Acknowledgements

This book was an easy decision to put together! I receive messages from my Instagram followers saying how I inspire them to improve their self-esteem, improve their health, exercising without excuses, so my first thank you is a BIG one to all my followers, who create this environment where I keep being inspired to create more quotes and more content to make you all feel fabulous about yourselves! I'd like to thank all the women in my life that helped shape me to be the woman that I am today.

I want to start with my mom, Rose Mesquita who taught me since I was a little girl to love myself and respect others. That is a lesson I take very seriously! Thank you to my big sister Vivianne Mesquita for being the true big sister in my life, always protecting me and making sure I am safe and happy! A big thank to my daughter Bella Wierson, who gives me feedback on my Instagram account and has also brought a few of her friends to follow me, which keeps me on my toes, to make sure I always send the very best message I can for all those girls! Hopefully they are already inspiring other girls in their lives!

I would need an entire book to thank all the amazing girlfriends that are and were part of my life! It never ceases to amaze me that sometimes we meet people as adults and feel like we've known them our entire life! I have to thank a couple of them here because they are directly connected to this project of mine: Thank you Julie Spangler for telling me that when I have an idea in my head, that I just need to start doing it, instead of waiting for all the ducks to be in a row! You inspire me every day, with the way you honor your values, your professionalism and wisdom, and more than anything, your friendship! Sundra Stockl, you are the loving friend every woman should have! You REALLY care! And I think I can say it without a doubt that you are my number one follower on Instagram, who always made me feel that this project meant something!

And instead of only thanking women, I'd like to thank my amazing husband Todd Peterson, who makes me feel fabulous every day! He is for sure a big part of my inspiration when I write some of the quotes, principally the ones about relationship! He also helped me edit this book with the many little grammar mistakes a Brazilian would make in a book written in a different language other than my native one. Te amo meu amor!

**Start NOW rewriting your own life story! Believe in yourself because you CAN! Don't just dream, TAKE ACTION and become the best version of yourself! But remember this: tiny steps is OK and lots of action is a MUST!**